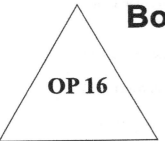

Boots on the Ground:
Troop Density
in Contingency
Operations

by
John J. McGrath

D1318909

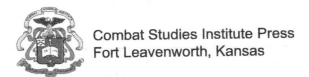

Combat Studies Institute Press
Fort Leavenworth, Kansas

Library of Congress Cataloging-in-Publication Data

McGrath, John J., 1956-
  Boots on the ground : troop density in contingency operations / by
John J. McGrath.
    p. cm. -- (Global war on terrorism occasional paper ; 16)
  Includes bibliographical references.
  1. Deployment (Strategy)--Case studies.   I. Title. II. Series.
U163.M392 2006
355.4--dc22

                                                2006012720

CSI Press publications cover a variety of military history topics. The views expressed
in this CSI Press publication are those of the author and not necessarily those of the
Department of the Army or the Department of Defense.

A full list of CSI Press publications, many of them available for downloading, can
be found at http://www.cgsc.army.mil/carl/resources/csi/csi.asp.

For sale by the Superintendent of Documents, U.S. Government Printing Office
Internet: bookstore.gpo.gov   Phone: toll free (866) 512-1800;   DC area (202) 512-1800
Fax: (202) 512-2250 Mail: Stop IDCC, Washington, DC 20402-0001

ISBN 0-16-076199-9

Foreword

John McGrath's *Troop Density* is a very timely historical analysis. While the value of history is indeed timeless, this paper clearly shows the immediate relevancy of historical study to current events. One of the most common criticisms of the US plan to invade Iraq in 2003 is that too few troops were used. The argument often fails to satisfy anyone for there is no standard against which to judge. Too few troops compared to what? Too few troops compared to which historical analogy? Too few troops compared to which policy maker's or which retired general's book?

A figure of 20 troops per 1000 of the local population is often mentioned as the standard, but as Mr. McGrath shows, that figure was arrived at with some questionable assumptions. By analyzing seven military operations in the last 100+ years, he arrives at an average number of military forces per 1000 of the population that have been employed in what would generally be considered successful military campaigns. He also points out a variety of important factors that affected those numbers – from peak troop levels, to geography, to local forces employed to supplement US troops, to the use of contractors – among many others.

A segment of American military historians and policy makers has been and is enamored with a genre of military history that seeks to quantify war, reduce it to known variables, and posit solutions to future military conflicts based on mathematical formulae. The practice of war contains a strong element of math, science, and social science, but in the end, the practice of war is an art. The numbers and percentages in this study are merely historical averages, with all the dangers inherent in any average figure. This study cannot be used to guarantee victory simply by putting a certain number of soldiers on the ground relative to the indigenous population. One would do well to remember that old adage about the six-foot tall statistician who drowned in the river that was *on average* only five feet deep.

It would also be tempting to seize upon Mr. McGrath's analysis and brandish it as a club with which to beat one's opponents in the current debate over troop levels in Operation Iraqi Freedom. This study should not be used in that way. As the author notes in *Appendix C: A Special Note on Iraq*, there are several reasons not to jump to definitive conclusions in the midst of this ongoing war. The number and effectiveness of Iraqi Security Forces have been steadily increasing since the summer of 2004. This creates a continually increasing troop density ratio in a struggle whose outcome is not yet known. Appendix C was added to this study as it went to print precisely to include the very latest numbers in this complex, evolving conflict. Poorly reasoned, presumptive judgments may very well be proved wrong by events.

Policy makers, commanders, and staff officers should use the numbers in this study as a guide, a basis from which to begin their analysis of the particular campaign at hand. They will still have to apply their understanding of the objectives, the nature of the conflict, and local and regional culture and conditions to the analysis in *Troop Density* to create a winning military plan. It is our belief at the CSI that this kind historical analysis will inform and educate today's military and civilian leaders as they carry out our nation's most important policies. *CSI—The Past is Prologue.*

Timothy R. Reese
Colonel, Armor
Director, Combat Studies Institute

Acknowledgments

This work marks my first GWOT Occasional Paper and my first foray into the field of quantitative analysis of military history. Like my previous topic selections, Dr. W. Glenn Robertson, US Army Combined Arms Center Chief Historian inspired this effort. Dr. Robertson discovered a void in the historical analysis of troop deployment size and he gave me the ball to run with and to develop such an analysis. Despite the quantitative nature of this work, I must advise the reader that the mathematics used is of the elementary level, familiar even to most historians like myself.

I must acknowledge the pioneer of quantitative analysis of military history, the late Colonel Trevor Dupuy, US Army retired. Through his many books and articles, he virtually created the genre to which this work is but a humble addition. While the execution of military operations is clearly an art, Colonel Dupuy illustrated how historical analysis of such operations may also be a science. I would also like to acknowledge other recent contributors to this field including retired Command Sergeant Major Robert Rush of the US Army Center of Military History and Niklas Zetterling of the Swedish National Defense College.

Research and Publications Team Chief Lieutenant Colonel Steve Clay provided outstanding guidance and support to this project. Colonel Timothy Reese, Director of the Combat Studies Institute, also provided continuous support, guidance, and advice. Mike Brooks, my editor on previous projects, provided critical guidance concerning the graphics on this project. Each colleague at the Combat Studies Institute has contributed to some extent the success of this effort.

Contributing greatly to the successful completion of this project is editor and OIF veteran Angela Bowman, whose skill at wordcraft is evident in every line of this work.

Finally, I would like to acknowledge the soldiers of the United States Army, whose superb efforts will hopefully be helped in some small way by this work.

John J. McGrath
Combat Studies Institute
Fort Leavenworth, Kansas

Contents

Figures

Tables

Chapter 1
Introduction

Recent Global War on Terrorism (GWOT) operations in Iraq have focused attention on the issue of the number of deployed troops needed to effectively conduct contingency operations. While pundits, military observers, and serving officers frequently address this issue, there seems to be no concise, systematic approach to this subject. Planning factors appear to be either extremely vague or nonexistent. Since historical analysis can be used to seek out examples from past similar operations to determine trends or estimates based on historical precedent, this work fills that gap with a brief but intensive study of troop strength in past contingency operations.

While there are no established rules for determining troop density, since 1995 several military observers, analysts, and civilian journalists have promulgated general theories on troop density. Most theorists generally cite historical precedent when proposing ratios for troop density levels. Most density recommendations fall within a range of 25 soldiers per 1000 residents in an area of operations (1 soldier per 40 inhabitants) to 20 soldiers per 1000 inhabitants (or 1 soldier per 50 inhabitants). The 20 to 1000 ratio is often considered the minimum effective troop density ratio.[1]

However, are these estimates supported by historical data? This work will study a selected sample of successful military contingency operations to answer that question. Scenarios, like Vietnam, that were not clearly defined as either a conventional or a contingency operation, and the success of which is still debated, will not be considered. Several smaller operations, such as Haiti, Grenada, the Dominican Republic, and other similarly ambiguous operations like Algeria, Panama, and Somalia will also be excluded from this analysis. In addition, since many of the activities of military forces in contingency operations are similar to the daily functions of civilian police forces, this work will also consider size and density factors for police forces. Accordingly, a review of the organization and deployable strength of several large municipal and state police forces in the United States will determine if there are any discernible planning factors used when deploying these forces.

Finally, a comprehensive analysis of all areas will be conducted to determine trends and commonalities. The analysis will then provide a recommended planning estimate for future contingency operations based on this review of historical experience in similar operations. The current operation in Iraq will be analyzed using the recommended planning estimate.

Additionally, this analysis will look at US troop strength planning estimates made prior to the Iraqi operation in relation to past similar operations.

Factors Involved in Determining Troop Density

The size of an area where troops will be conducting contingency operations and the population density of the area are key factors in determining troop density. For example, the greater the number of troops and the smaller the geographic area of responsibility, the greater the likelihood a contingency operation will succeed. In this work, historical examples will be examined to determine if this logical assumption is accurate and to determine any trends in troop deployment strength based on geography and demographics.

Various types of geographical settings may affect decisions regarding troop density. For example, while the land mass of the Philippines is 115,000 square miles, this mass covers an area of 700,000 square miles and consists of over 460 islands larger than one square mile and 11 islands larger than 1000 square miles. The noncontiguous nature of the land area of this archipelago would, therefore, require more troops and more separate detachments than a contiguous area of similar size not separated by bodies of water. While densely populated urban and suburban areas will require a greater troop density (and will be analyzed both as part of a larger example and separately), large, underpopulated areas with covering terrain such as jungles, forests, or mountains may require more troops than an analysis of the population density alone may indicate. Covering terrain provides ideal assembly areas and sanctuaries for insurgents, terrorists, and foreign adventurers. For the purposes of this work, however, geographical variations (except for population density) will be studied by exception and only as necessary.

In addition to population density, specifics of demographics may play a significant role in troop density considerations. Dr. Richard Stewart has rightfully pointed out the number of young adult males and the unemployment rate may be key factors to consider when determining troop density.[2] However, detailed demographic analysis is beyond the scope of this work. Nontraditional demographic models will be analyzed in this work only by exception, as necessary, to help explain anomalies in the analysis.

Mission and Roles

Major contingency operations are a bundle of closely related operational, civil affairs, and police-type activities. Table 1 lists the functions of contingency operations as outlined in US Army Field Manual (FM) 7-30, *The Infantry Brigade:*[3]

Table 1. Types of Contingency Operations

Type	Missions
Peace Operations	**Peacekeeping:** employ patrols, establish checkpoints, roadblocks, buffer zones, supervise truce, EPW exchange, reporting and monitoring, negotiation and mediation, liaison, investigation of complaints and violations, civil disturbance missions, and offensive and defensive missions.
	Peace Enforcement: separate belligerents; establish and supervise protected zones, sanction enforcement, movement denial and guarantee, restoration and maintenance of order, area security, humanitarian assistance, civil disturbance missions, and offensive and defensive missions.
	Operations in Support of Diplomatic Efforts: conduct military-to-military contacts, conduct exercises, provide security assistance, restore civil authority, rebuild physical infrastructure, provide structures and training for schools and hospitals, and reestablish commerce.
Foreign Internal Defense	**Indirect Support:** military-to-military contacts, exercises, area security.
	Direct Support: civil-military operations, intelligence and communications sharing, and logistical support.
	Combat Operations: offensive and defensive missions.
Support to Insurgencies	Show of force, defensive missions, raids, area security, employ patrols, and provide Combat Service Support.

(continued on next page)

Table 1. Types of Contingency Operations

Type	Mission
Counterdrug Operations	Liaison and advisor duty, civic action, intelligence support, surveillance support, reconnaissance, logistical support, and information support.
Combating Terrorism	Conduct force protection, offensive and defensive missions.
Noncombatant Evacuation Operations	Attack to seize terrain that secures evacuees or departure area, guard, convoy security, delay, and defend.
Arms Control	Seize and destroy weapons, convoy escort, assist and monitor inspection of arms, and conduct surveillance.
Show of Force	Perform tactical movement, demonstration, defensive operations, and perform training exercises.
Domestic Civil Disturbance Operations	Assist law enforcement activities and security operations.

The above figure illustrates how the functions of contingency operations are varied and often specialized. However, for the purposes of determining general troop densities in such operations, this analysis presumes a troop deployment will primarily consist of general purpose forces that can be either retrained quickly or reoriented to conduct specific functions.

In addition to the various missions soldiers conduct during contingency operations, a deployed force includes troops employed in command and control, and administrative and logistic functions. As with the varied demographic factors, these supporting elements will not be discussed in this analysis unless required by exception.

External Factors

This work will use past military and civilian police experience to develop planning factors or estimates for troop densities in contingency operations. However, in many cases, external factors affected troop densities and the result was deployment numbers either greater than or fewer than ideal. For example, political considerations may affect the size of a deployed force. In the Philippines from 1899 to 1901, for instance, the number of deployed troops was twice reduced, based not on military considerations, but solely on the desire to expeditiously return volunteer soldiers to civilian life at the end of their enlistments. In this work, the role of external factors will be discussed as necessary as part of the analysis of the historical record of troop density in contingency operations.

Methodology

In order to determine the number of troops needed for future contingency operations, this analysis contains five sections. First, past successful contingency operations are analyzed based on geographical area, terrain, population density, troop deployment and organization, and indigenous support. Second, the size and organization of various municipal and state police departments in the United States will be reviewed individually and then in comparison with each other. Third, the accumulated data will be analyzed using several factors including population density, troop availability, recruitment and rotation, intensity and duration of the conflict, police versus military troop densities, and the relative importance of indigenous and substitute forces in the conduct of the operation. Fourth, the above information will be synthesized to identify trends in determining troop densities in past contingency operations and to formulate recommended troop levels for estimating deployment densities in future contingency operations. This is a brief analysis of a complex issue. For a more in-depth study, additional research would be required. However, this work offers an immediate answer to the question of how many troops should be deployed for successful conduct of a contingency operation.

Contingency operations are complex and vary in intensity and scope, making comparisons between past operations possibly problematic. However, for the purposes of this study, the historical examples used are considered equal in scope and intensity, although intensity will be analyzed as one of the factors when the various historical examples are compared with each other. Additionally, troop quality can vary among regular serving soldiers, indigenous forces, substitute forces (such as contractors), and police. For the purposes of this study, soldier quality is assumed to be equal for all operational forces serving in a full time status.

Notes

1.   Stephen Budiansky, "Formula for How Many Troops We Need," *Washington Post,* 9 May 2004, B04 [article on-line] available at http://www.spokesmanre view.com/breaking-news-story.asp?submitdate=2004510151143; Internet; accessed 13 January 2005; Daniel Smith, "Iraq: Descending into the Quagmire," *Foreign Policy In Focus Policy Report,* June 2003 [document on-line] available at http:// www.fpif.org/papers/quagmire2003.html; Internet; accessed 9 November 2005; Kevin Drum, "Political Animal: Not Enough Troops in Iraq?" *Washington Monthly,* 9 January 2005 [article on-line] available at http://www.washingtonmonthly.com/ar chives/individual/2005_01/005422.php; Internet; accessed 14 January 2005; James Quinlivan, "Burden of Victory: The Painful Arithmetic of Stability Operations," *Rand Review,* 27 no. 3 (Summer 2003) 18 August 2005 [article on-line] available at http://www.rand.org/publications/randreview/issues/summer2003/burden.html; Internet; accessed 14 September 2005; James Quinlivan, "Force Requirements in Stability Operations," *Parameters,* 23 (Winter 1995), 59-69.

2.   Richard Stewart, "Occupations Then and Now." In *Armed Diplomacy: Two Centuries of American Campaigning* (paper presented at conference sponsored by the US Army Training and Doctrine Command, Fort Leavenworth, KS, 5-7 August 2003), (Fort Leavenworth: Combat Studies Institute Press, 2004), 272.

3.   Department of the Army, FM 7-30, *The Infantry Brigade,* change 1 dated 31 October 2000 (Washington, DC: Department of the Army, 3 October 1995), Table J-7, p. J-34. FM 7-30 uses the term stability operations when describing what this work refers to as contingency operations. The current dictionary of Army operational terms (FM 1-02, *Operational Terms and Graphics,* September 2004) only contains the term stability operations. For the purposes of this work, stability and contingency operations will be synonymous.

Chapter 2

Historical Examples

The Philippines, 1899-1901

Situational Narrative

In May 1898 as part of global operations in the Spanish-American War, a small American naval force under Commodore (later Rear Admiral) George Dewey defeated a Spanish naval squadron based in Manila Bay in the Spanish colony of the Philippines, an archipelago in the Pacific Ocean off the East Asian coast. Following Dewey's success, Major General Wesley Merritt led a 5000-soldier expedition to secure the base at Manila. Merritt subsequently received reinforcements and his command was designated the Eighth Corps. With these reinforcements, he attacked the Spanish position at Manila and captured the city in August 1898. Meanwhile Filipinos, led by former insurgent leader Emilio Aguinaldo, who the United States had recently returned from exile in Hong Kong, revolted against the Spanish. Aguinaldo's forces played a supporting role in the capture of Manila. While the American forces, now led by Major General Elwell S. Otis, held an enclave around Manila throughout the last half of 1898 awaiting the results of peace negotiations with the Spanish, Aguinaldo organized an "army of liberation" and an independent Filipino government.

When the 10 December 1898 Treaty of Paris ceded the Philippines to the United States, conflict with Aguinaldo and his forces became inevitable.[1] Hostilities between the Filipino forces and Otis' troops formally began in early February 1899. The conventional phase of operations lasted until the end of that year and primarily centered on the largest and most populous island of Luzon. While early US successes included securing the area around Manila, the redeployment in mid-1899 of almost half of his force, most of whom were limited-term volunteers, hindered Otis' ability to execute offensive operations.

Over a period of several months, an expanded Regular Army force and a newly raised force of 24 US national volunteer regiments gradually replaced these troops. With these reinforcements, Otis renewed offensive operations, focusing on Aguinaldo's stronghold in northern Luzon. These successful actions from October through December 1899 forced Aguinaldo to declare an end to conventional fighting and revert to a guerilla campaign. Simultaneously, under the terms of the peace treaty, the remaining small Spanish garrisons prepared to leave the outlying islands of the archipelago. Fearing the void, which had already been filled in many areas by Aguinaldo supporters or allies, Otis deployed forces throughout the archipelago in early 1900, extending the geographical arena for operations across the full 7100 islands and 115,000 square miles of the former Spanish possession.[2] The War Department and Otis formalized the shift to contingency operations in April 1900 by discontinuing the Eighth Corps and setting up a geographically based Military Division of the Philippines, with four subordinate departments, each containing multiple districts. Department and district commanders and their subordinate commanders had both operational and civil affairs functions. Otis was both the commander of the military division and the military governor of the Philippines.[3]

With this new structure, stability operations were conducted on a decentralized, local level with great success in 1900 and 1901, continuing after Major General Arthur MacArthur replaced Otis in May 1900. During this time, the insurgency gradually declined, culminating in the capture of Aguinaldo in March 1901 and his subsequent appeal for a cessation of hostilities. By mid-1901 major resistance was limited to the Batangas Province of Luzon and the island of Samar.[4] At about the same time, a smaller, Regular Army force replaced the national volunteer regiments that then redeployed and mustered out of federal service. Major General Adna Chaffee replaced MacArthur in July 1901. Limited hostilities continued until President Theodore Roosevelt officially declared them over as of 4 July 1902.

Geographical Area, Terrain, and Population Density

In 1899 the Philippines was an archipelago of over 7000 islands, with 460 islands larger than one square mile and only 11 islands larger than 1000 square miles. The land area was 115,000 square miles. At that time, over 90 percent of the population lived on the largest 11 islands and totaled about seven million.[5] Most of the 11 large islands contained at least one large urban area; Manila on Luzon was the largest urban area. Terrain away from the cities varied from rugged mountainous areas to forests, jungles, open plains, and agricultural areas where rice and hemp were the predominate crops. Overall, the climate was tropical.

In 1899, 2.8 million people, or approximately one-third of the Filipino population, lived on Luzon, the largest, northernmost island.[6] Aside from being the most densely populated island, Luzon was also the most militarily significant, containing the city of Manila and the heart of the Filipino insurgency. The leaders of the insurgency were predominately from the Tagalog ethnic group on Luzon. Filipino population density throughout the islands was about 61 persons per square mile. However, in the more densely populated regions of central and northern Luzon, this rose to 67 persons per square mile.

US Troop Deployment and Organization

Otis, then US commander in the Philippines, wrote to the Adjutant General in Washington in August 1899 stating he felt no more than 50,000 troops could successfully quell the Philippine Insurrection and conduct occupation duties. Otis felt an additional 15,000 troops would be needed if the insurrection spread to the southern islands of Jolo and Mindanao. His force at the time numbered about 30,000, with projected reinforcements of 10,000. This total included 12 US national volunteer regiments recently raised specifically for service in the archipelago. To meet his demand for more troops, Otis requested and received approval for the creation of an additional 15 regiments of national volunteers for garrison duty in the islands.[7] Otis based these figures on his military knowledge, garnered from his career, which began in the large mass armies of the Civil War and extended for decades in the frontier Army. At the time of his estimate, Filipino insurgents still fielded a substantial conventional force, so Otis based his figures on defeating that force, the need to conduct any subsequent guerilla operations, and garrisoning the archipelago.

While the southern regions would, to some extent, ultimately join the insurrection, Otis and his successors would deploy far less than the projected 15,000 soldiers to those areas, giving the departmental commander of Mindanao and Jolo at most 2600 soldiers.[8] However, theater-wide, peak deployment would exceed Otis' maximum estimate of 65,000, reaching 68,816 in October 1900. Troop strength would remain above 60,000 during the peak months of the guerilla campaign from January to December 1900.[9] Additionally, the troop strength numbers were greatest following the defeat of Aguinaldo's conventional forces. Figure 1 illustrates monthly US troop strength numbers.

Even though a large component of the deployed force consisted of nonprofessional volunteers, these troops proved to be very effective. Their high level of training and professionalism meant, in practical terms, there was no distinction between their operational deployment and employment and that of the recently expanded Regular Army. However, unlike the regulars, the volunteers had a limited tour of service. Table 2 depicts troop density, geography data, and troop strength numbers for the Philippine Insurrection.

As can be seen from table 2, US soldiers were spread thin throughout the archipelago, averaging slightly more than one soldier for every two square miles of territory, and 1 soldier for a little over 100 Filipino

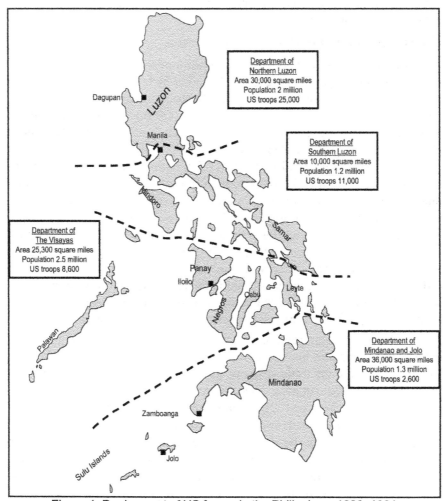

Figure 1. Deployment of US forces in the Philippines, 1899–1901

inhabitants. However, US commanders did not deploy these soldiers evenly throughout the islands. As previously cited, the majority of the garrison was **deployed on Luzon, specifically in the northern Luzon area, where the troop** density averaged more than 1.5 soldiers per two square miles and about 10 soldiers per 1000 residents. In fact, the relative importance of Luzon is apparent in the deployment of 35,000 US troops, a little over half of all US forces deployed to the Philippines, to the island at the peak of US troop strength.[10] Figure 2 illustrates the troop deployment allocations of the Military Division of the Philippines in 1900.

Table 2. Troop Density in the Philippine Insurrection

Area	Military Forces (at maximum)	Population	Area (square miles)	Population Density (per square mile)	Soldier Density		Soldiers Per 1000 Residents
					Per Area (soldiers per square mile)	Per Population (one soldier per x residents) $x=$	
Philippines 1899-1901	68,816	7,000,000	115,000	60.90	0.59	101.70	9.80
Northern Luzon 1899-1901	25,000	2,000,000	30,000	66.70	0.83	80.00	12.50

11

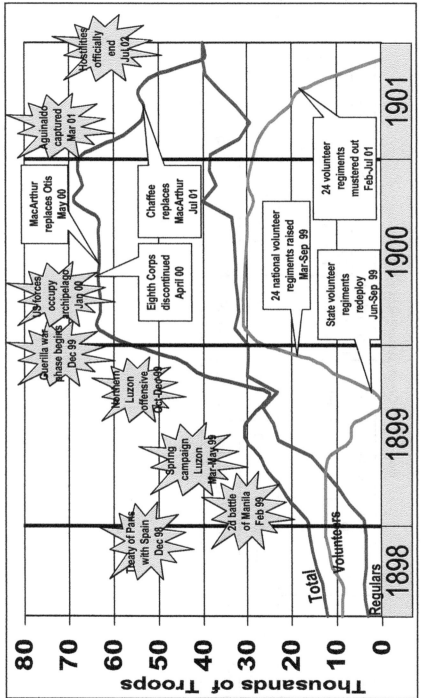

Figure 2. US forces in the Philippines, 1898-1901.

The initial estimate for the number of troops required as garrison forces during the post-insurrection phase was 40,000 Regular Army troops, including 30,000 infantry, 9000 cavalry, 8 companies of coast artillery, 2 field artillery batteries, and 3 mountain artillery batteries.[11] However, despite the outbreak of a new insurrection among the Moslem Moros of southern Mindanao in 1902, the size of the US garrison in the Philippines soon fell below the 40,000 figure to approximately 23,000 by 1903.[12]

Indigenous Support

The recruitment of Filipino forces to support US stability operations during the insurrection began slowly in 1900 when MacArthur expanded the role of the preexisting Filipino police and established a force of native scouts. These forces together numbered about 3400 in May 1900.[13] Though relatively small in numbers, the friendly Filipino forces often spearheaded or assisted in US counterinsurgency operations, particularly in the latter stages of the insurgency.

Conclusion

While operating with minimal indigenous support over a period of less than three years, American forces subdued insurrection in the Philippines by employing an area troop density of 0.59 soldiers per square mile throughout the archipelago and a population troop density of 9.8 soldiers per 1000 inhabitants. In the sections of Luzon where insurgent activity was most intense, US forces were more concentrated, and the troop density ratio for the area equated to 0.83 soldiers per square mile and a population to troop density ratio of 12.5 soldiers per 1000 Northern Luzon inhabitants.

Postwar Germany

Situational Narrative

As early as 1942, Allied staff officers began preparing for the postwar occupation of Germany, a projected mission made an operational necessity when the Allies demanded Germany's unconditional surrender at the January 1943 Casablanca Conference. After the presumed surrender of Germany, the Allied powers (the United States, Great Britain, and the Soviet Union) intended to occupy the entire territorial expanse of Germany until civil German government was reestablished. The Allied powers did not identify an end date or duration for the occupation. The amount of resistance expected from the German populace and former military elements was unknown, but Allied combat troops would be available initially in sufficient numbers if such resistance appeared. At the Yalta Conference, President Franklin D. Roosevelt stated the United States politically could only field an occupation force in Germany for two years. However, most planners considered five years to be a more realistic minimum duration estimate.[14]

Not anticipating future animosity from Soviet dictator Joseph Stalin, US planners intended to leave the minimum necessary force in Germany to conduct stability and reconstruction operations. The remainder of the force would redeploy from Germany to the Pacific to help defeat Japan or back to the United States for discharge. Operation Plan (OPLAN) ECLIPSE detailed occupation responsibilities and national sectors of those forces remaining in Germany. At the end of the war, US troops occupied large areas of the projected British, French, and Soviet sectors as well as the entire projected US sector. This necessitated a US troop withdrawal into the American sector by July 1945. The redeployment of US troops from the Soviet sector was delayed until the Soviets agreed to withdraw from the portions of Berlin previously designated as British, French, and American occupation sectors.[15]

Even though 780,372 soldiers quickly deployed out of the theater for service in the Pacific, over two million troops remained to conduct occupation duties. This, coupled with the complete defeat of enemy military forces and the destruction of the Nazi government apparatus, resulted in US forces adopting a system of blanket or "army" occupation.[16] Under this system, US units deployed throughout the American sector to conduct occupation duties, and corps and divisions assumed responsibility for specific German counties (*Landkreise*).

With the surrender of Japan in August 1945 and the subsequent rapid demobilization of troops, it soon became apparent the Army could not continue to support the army-type occupation; military government officers preferred a less dense style of occupation. Therefore, beginning in October 1945, the US forces in Germany gradually adopted a style of occupation similar to that implemented in Japan, the so-called police-type occupation. In this kind of occupation, the preexisting Japanese police force remained in place to conduct law and order operations under American supervision, backed up by US tactical units consolidated in regiment-size cantonments.[17]

In Germany, where the police force was nonexistent or was tainted with the brush of Nazism, converted American units formed the equivalent force. By 1 July 1946 the 4th Armored Division and the remaining mechanized cavalry groups in Germany reorganized as the US Constabulary, with a total strength of about 30,000 troopers. The Constabulary was designed specifically for policing postwar Germany and guarding the new border with the Soviet zone. Apart from the Constabulary, by September 1947 the Army retained only one infantry division and several separate infantry battalions and companies in Germany with a total strength, including the Constabulary, of 117,224 soldiers. From January 1947 until November 1950, the strength of the US ground forces in Germany remained between 91,000 and 117,000 soldiers.[18]

Different authorities cite various time frames for the actual duration of the occupation. Officially, it lasted until March 1955 when the Treaty of Paris formally established West German sovereignty. However, after the 1948 Berlin Airlift, the nature of the occupation gradually shifted into a defense of Europe against the Soviets, as opposed to oversight of the German recovery, and the Constabulary gradually transformed back into a standard tactical organization. The political and economic unification of the French, British, and US sectors into the Federal Republic of Germany in 1949 was the next major step. However, the communist invasion of South Korea in June 1950 marked the real beginning of the end of the occupation. The subsequent American troop build-up in Germany, which began in November 1950 with the reactivation of the 7th Army headquarters, clearly marked the shift away from occupation to defense. For the purposes of this work, therefore, November 1950 will mark the end of the occupation.

The occupation of Germany posed unique problems not generally seen in other occupations or contingency operations. While there was no insurgency, troops not only had to police large areas of Germany, they also had to fight black marketeering, and support, guard, and process hundreds of thousands of prisoners of war and 2.5 million displaced persons (DP).[19] Additionally, millions of dollars of American and captured materiel had to be guarded and disposed of. During the occupation, the United States had to redeploy a large contingent to fight the Japanese, and then later redeploy a significant number of soldiers to the United States for discharge and return to civilian life, while maintaining a suitably sized occupation force. Simultaneously, a large portion of the occupying force had to be retrained and converted into the Constabulary.

Another unique aspect of the occupation was the arrival of American dependent family members beginning in May 1946. The arrival of families meant the creation of permanent quarters and garrison posts and was a key indicator the occupation was transforming into a permanent defensive force for Western Europe.[20]

Geographical Area, Terrain, and Population Density

The initial sector of Germany allocated to the United States for occupation purposes consisted of the German state of Bavaria in the east, and what later became the state of Hesse in the north and the northern portion of the state of Baden-Württemberg in the west.[21] Original US planning figures estimated the US occupation zone of Germany to be 45,600 square miles and to contain a population of 17.8 million.[22] Thus, the proposed occupation zone had a population density of 372.8 inhabitants per square mile. While the French assumed part of the original zone in July 1945, later figures, including prisoners of war, refugees, and DPs, estimated the population to be about 19 million, or a population density of 416.7 persons per square mile. The US zone also included a sector in Berlin and a small enclave at the port of Bremerhaven in the British sector. Bremerhaven provided the main port and supply hub for the US forces in Germany. The US occupation zone in Austria will be discussed separately.[23]

Army-Type Occupation Force

On V-E Day, 8 May 1945, there were 1,622,000 US troops in Germany organized into 59 divisions, 15 corps, 5 armies, and 2 army groups. The total theater force was 3,069,310.[24] This force had been assembled to defeat the Germans. However, only a small number were earmarked for subsequent occupation duties, while up to 1.5 million were designated for immediate transfer to the Pacific and another 600,000 to be sent back to the United States for discharge as excess. By July 1945 the two army group headquarters and one army headquarters had been disbanded and 1 army headquarters, 3 corps headquarters, and 11 divisions had redeployed to the continental United States for service either in the invasion of Japan or as a strategic reserve.[25]

As originally conceived in OPLAN ECLIPSE, the occupation force would be a strong force capable of responding to all contingencies, later referred to as the army-type occupation force. The required strength of this force, called the Occupational Troop Basis (OTB), was determined to be 404,500. Originally, this would include 2 army headquarters, 3 corps headquarters, and 10 divisions that would be in place within a year and a half following the German surrender. The army-type occupation force would rely on conventional tactical units to serve as the occupation force.[26]

The sudden defeat of Japan in August 1945 resulted in the reduction of the OTB for the occupation of Germany long before it could be implemented. The projected strength was decreased to 370,000, and eight divisions. Three divisions would be in Bavaria (which later became the Western [then

16

First] Military District), four in Hesse and Baden-Württemberg (which together became the Eastern [then Second] Military District) and a division (minus) in Berlin with one of its regiments in Bremerhaven. One armored combat command and one paratrooper regiment were earmarked as a mobile reserve. The rest of the OTB force would be concentrated in regiment-size units at various posts. The deadline for OTB implementation was shortened from a year and a half to one year.[27]

In addition to the OTB, an additional 337,000 troops were designated to be in place by July 1946 to guard and liquidate over six million tons of excess and captured materiel located in the American zone. By July 1946 the total force, including the OTB and those soldiers designated to liquidate materiel, was projected to be 707,000. A clear indication this required figure was not seriously considered is the fact that as early as the end of December 1945, total troop strength in Germany was 93,000 less than the 614,000 projected for July 1946. New projections counted the number of divisions rather than the total number of troops, with the total projected force reduced from eight to less than five divisions by the end of June 1946 and further reductions after that date. However, even these projections would prove to be overly optimistic because concurrent with these reductions, the Army was adopting a new theory of occupation force size in Japan that would require even fewer troops.[28]

Police-Type Occupation Force

Within several months following the Japanese surrender, the OTB would be radically reduced. A new occupation theory, called the police-type occupation, was developed to cope with both the lack of a strong German resistance and the fact that concurrent rapid demobilization would soon result in the unavailability of a large force.[29]

The theory behind the police-type occupation was for a highly mobile, highly trained police-style force to maintain primary control of the occupied area. Once formed, this force, the US Constabulary, would patrol the American zone and the border with the Soviet zone much like police forces in the United States patrolled cities and states. A mobile combat force of three divisions stationed in centrally located, regiment-size concentrations would back up the Constabulary. Military government planners determined the authorized size of the Constabulary at 38,000 by using the rough estimate of providing one Constabulary trooper for every 450 Germans, using prewar census figures to determine the German population. This provided a ratio of 2.2 Constabulary soldiers per 1000 German inhabitants.[30] The projected end-strength of the OTB for the police-type

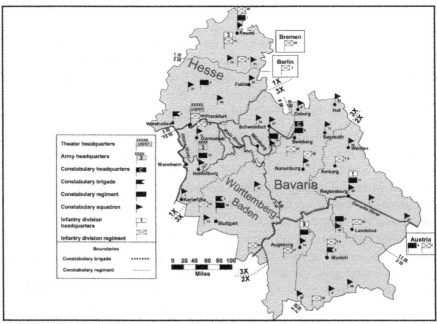

Figure 3. Organization of the American zone, July 1946.

occupation force was 203,000, including the Constabulary, one army head-quarters (Third Army), three divisions (1st, 3d, and 9th Infantry Divisions) and the previously excluded occupation forces in the adjacent US zone in Austria.[31] **The police-type occupation was projected to last five years and** the Constabulary was scheduled for inactivation by 1 July 1950.[32]

By 1 July 1946 the 4th Armored Division and the remaining theater cavalry groups reorganized into the Constabulary, made up of three brigades of three regiments each. One brigade was responsible for one each of the three German states located in the American zone based on area. Constabulary squadrons deployed across the zone and along the border with the Soviet zone, while the three-division tactical force deployed in regiment-size concentrations across the American zone. Figure 3 depicts the organization of the American zone in Germany in July 1946.

Concurrent with the adoption of the police-type occupation force, demobilization and drawdown rapidly continued. The 316,000-member closeout force, whose mission it was to liquidate stocks of surplus or cap-tured equipment, redeployed over the first half of 1946. The Constabulary would never reach its target strength of 38,000, attaining a maximum size of only 33,076 before demands for an even smaller occupation force af-fected its strength.[33]

Upon becoming operational in July 1946, the Constabulary's 27 squadrons were arrayed throughout the sector with a brigade of three regiments (nine squadrons per brigade) in each of the three states of the American zone. The three-division tactical force was consolidated primarily into regiment-size groupings, with the 3d Infantry Division in Hesse and northern Baden, the 9th Infantry Division in southwestern Bavaria and northern Württemberg, and the 1st Infantry Division in western and northern Bavaria. A separate infantry regiment garrisoned Bremen and Berlin. However, the continued downsizing would soon transform this scheme.

After July 1946 the pace of the drawdown slowed. In September the OTB for July 1947 was reduced to 117,000, including the Austrian occupation force. The three-division mobile combat force was reduced first to two and then to a single division.[34] Completing the move from a tactical to a police-style system, Third Army headquarters was inactivated in March 1947 and the Constabulary headquarters assumed most of its functions.[35] By June 1947, two years into the occupation, actual troop strength stood at 117,224, including 11,345 troops in Austria.[36] The Constabulary was reduced in size soon after its establishment. As part of a revised strength authorization of 18,000 by September 1947, the Constabulary was reduced by 1 brigade, 4 regiments, and 11 squadrons. The remaining elements were reorganized and spread out even farther across the US zone.[37] Figure 4 illustrates the reduction in force strength from 1945 to June 1947.

Concurrent with these reductions, the nature of the occupation began to change from police-type operations to defense from external threats. Tensions increased between the former western Allies and the Soviet Union, culminating in the Berlin Blockade in March 1948. The shift to a defensive posture began with the consolidation of a regiment of the 1st Infantry Division at the Grafenwöhr training area in late summer 1947. The 1st Infantry Division had served as the American tactical reserve force and had been widely dispersed across the zone after the departure of the other two divisions. At the same time, the increased role of the German police in local law enforcement allowed the Constabulary to function as an emergency reaction force or to provide police coverage for areas not under the German police. As a result, the 5th Constabulary Regiment consolidated at Augsburg simultaneous to the 1st Division's regimental concentration at Grafenwöhr.[38]

The 1948-49 Soviet blockade of West Berlin and the subsequent Berlin Airlift marked the beginning of the change in the mission of the Army in Europe from occupation to defense. This completed the reorientation of the Constabulary from a police to a tactical force. In December 1948 the

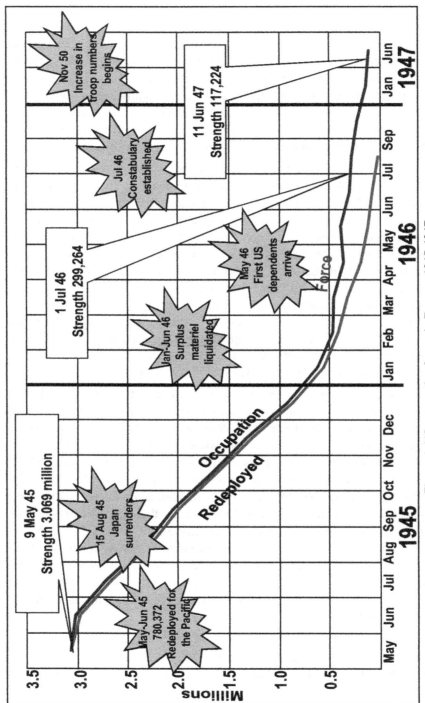

Figure 4. US occupation forces in Europe, 1945-1947.

Constabulary was accordingly reduced and reorganized into a two-brigade force. Under the brigades, three former regiments and nine squadrons converted to three armored cavalry regiments. The Army retained only two Constabulary squadrons, one in Berlin and one near the border with the Soviet zone. The Communist attack on South Korea in June 1950 finalized the shift from occupation to defense. The Constabulary headquarters converted into a reactivated Seventh Army headquarters on 24 November 1950.[39] This new defensive mission required a build-up of combat forces. Two corps headquarters, V Corps in June and VII Corps in October, and four divisions deployed to Germany from the United States between May and November 1951.[40]

Organization of the Occupation

Apart from the tactical units, a military community structure developed in Germany based on two decisions made in the fall of 1945: the plan to restation US forces in larger, regimental garrisons, and the decision to allow the dependents of occupation soldiers to live in the occupation areas. In April 1946 the construction of military communities, including family housing, commenced. Additionally, a system of schools for dependent children was established and various support facilities were created.

Following stateside practice, the communities were initially called military posts and sub-posts.[41] Each post command was responsible for a certain geographical area, and included all US installations in the area. With a small headquarters staff, colonels, typically the commander of the senior tactical unit in the area, commanded the military posts, which were similar in size to US counties. The post command conducted all administrative functions, leaving the tactical and Constabulary units free to execute their primary missions. Following German practice, several military posts were organized into military districts. In 1947 there were two military districts, one in the states of Hesse and Württemberg-Baden under the Headquarters, US Constabulary, and another in Bavaria under the headquarters of the 1st Infantry Division.[42] The districts controlled the military posts in their areas operationally, while European theater staff and units worked with each post directly to provide logistic and administrative support. Initially, there were 19 military posts in the American sector, illustrated in figure 5. The post of Frankfurt, staffed by the Army theater headquarters, US Forces, European Theater (USFET) and the post of Wiesbaden, staffed by the Army Air Force theater headquarters, US Air Force, Europe (USAFE), did not fall under any district. As the drawdown continued, posts were consolidated and the district headquarters were eliminated.[43]

Higher organization in the theater initially included two army headquarters, an army theater headquarters, and a parallel military government structure. The USFET commander was also the US Military Governor of Germany. As such, he commanded a separate military government organization, the Office of Military Government for Germany (US) or OMGUS. USFET was redesignated the European Command (EUCOM) in March 1947. EUCOM was a joint command, and in November 1947, a separate Army theater command was created under EUCOM called US Army, Europe (USAREUR).[44]

While initially soldiers in units who had fought the war together conducted the occupation, the demobilization process, based on individual replacements rather than unit replacements, soon transformed the occupation force units into a mix of individual fillers who had the lowest priority for demobilization. Over time, individual replacements refilled the force. While conceptually the Army's elite soldiers were to fill the

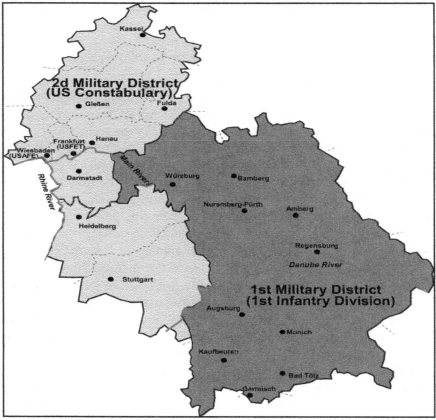

Figure 5. US occupation military districts, June 1947.

Constabulary's ranks, it too was filled with individual replacements who received no special training or selection.[45]

Austria

US forces also participated in the occupation of Austria. As in Germany, the United States occupied sectors, one around around Salzburg and one in the capital city of Vienna. The US zone in Austria covered an area of 6200 square miles and contained a population of 1,297,700.[46] Unlike Germany, occupation planning for Austria was initially marked by uncertainty concerning participation and troop levels. Initial estimates for Austria consisted of the projected deployment of a corps with one armored and two infantry divisions totaling 73,000 soldiers. This force would be in place for a period of time between 4 and 12 months after the end of the war, and then be downsized to a force of 28,000 with one division and a regimental combat team. Despite the projected requirements, the OTB for the Austria occupation was soon reduced to a starting figure of 28,030 soldiers and included a corps headquarters and one or two infantry divisions. This was further reduced to an occupation headquarters and one infantry division, still with a maximum strength of 28,000.[47]

In the first six months, the occupation troops deployed to Austria were in a state of constant flux. Initially, the XV Corps was responsible for the projected US zone in Austria, but in July 1945, the II Corps, with the 42d and 65th Infantry Divisions and the 11th Armored Division, replaced XV Corps. The XV Corps, part of the original blanket occupation, contained about 70,000 soldiers and included at various times the 101st Airborne Division, the 14th Armored Division, and the 83d and 26th Infantry Divisions. By the end of October 1945, the 83d Infantry Division had become the main element of the occupation force in Austria, with the 4th Cavalry Group attached. By early 1946 the occupation force was roughly 41,000 in size.

The 83d soon redeployed to the United States for inactivation, replaced by the separate 5th Infantry Regiment (April-November 1946) that was then replaced by the 1st Infantry Division's 16th Infantry Regiment (reduced to only two battalions). Concurrently, the 4th Cavalry Group was converted into the 4th Constabulary Regiment with two subordinate squadrons (the 4th and 24th). By June 1947, two years into the occupation, actual US troop strength in Austria was 1345 soldiers. In June 1948, the 1st Infantry Division was concentrated in Germany, and the 350th Infantry, formerly of the 88th Infantry Division, was reactivated to become the chief occupation force in Austria. The 350th remained in Austria until 1955 when the US occupation ended.[48]

Indigenous Support

Initially, civilian support to the American contingency operation was nonexistent in Germany. However, the revival of the German border police force in 1946 and the expansion and increased role of German police, both locally and along the zonal borders, released American forces for other missions or inactivation.

New German border police forces were established on a state basis in early 1946 to assist US forces in controlling the borders between the states and zones. The planned total size was 4000, a strength figure which was almost achieved by July 1946. With the activation of the Constabulary that same month, the border police were under the control of the new organization, instead of local civilian state governments as originally planned. The border police and local police gradually expanded as the Constabulary downsized.

In March 1947 the border police were rearmed and placed under the operational control of the US military government. The Germans soon assumed complete control over border patrol operations, culminating in August 1948 with the complete withdrawal of the Constabulary from the border.[49]

Concurrent with the development of the border police, the local police (*Landespolizei*) were organized on a state-by-state basis in 1946. The downsizing of the Constabulary in August 1947 led to the expansion of German police authority as the Germans assumed all local police functions for German nationals, while the Constabulary continued as an emergency reaction force and as the police force in areas not under German police jurisdiction. DPs and other foreigners remained under the jurisdiction of the Constabulary.[50]

In Austria the situation contrasted greatly with the situation in the American sector of Germany. The Soviets had established a civilian government almost as soon as their forces captured Vienna. This government was retained when US, British, and French forces subsequently joined the Soviets in the occupation of Austria. It ultimately evolved into the neutralist Austrian government, which attained full sovereignty in 1955.

As part of this civil government, federal and local police forces, established from the start, played an important role in local law enforcement from the early days of the occupation. The local Austrian forces numbered about 6000 police officers in the American sector in 1947.[51]

Table 3. Troop Density in the Occupation of Germany and Austria

	Military Forces (ground forces)	Population	Area (square miles)	Population Density (per square mile)	Soldier Density		
					Per Area (soldiers per square mile)	Per Population (one soldier per x residents) x=	Soldiers Per 1000 Residents
Germany, 1945-49		19,000,000	45,600	416.7			
Army occupation projected (maximum final size)	285,000				6.25	66.70	15.00
Police occupation projected (maximum final size)	203,000				4.45	93.60	10.68
Constabulary (projected)	38,000				0.83	500.00	2.00
Police occupation actual one year	299,264				6.56	63.50	15.75
Two years	117,224				2.57	162.10	6.16
Constabulary actual	33,076				0.72	574.43	1.74
Austria, 1945-49		1,297,700	6200	209.30			
Planned (maximum)	73,000				11.77	17.78	56.25
Actual two years (maximum)	11,345				1.83	114.39	8.74

Conclusion

Initial occupation planning estimates for one year following the German surrender projected a force of 21.28 soldiers per 1000 German inhabitants. The large army-type occupation plan was never fully implemented due to the adoption and implementation of the smaller, police-type occupation plan. At its maximum, the total force size of the police-type occupation was projected to be 203,000, or a ratio of 10.68 soldiers per 1000 inhabitants, roughly half the size of the army-type occupation. At the heart of the police-type occupation was the US Constabulary, whose projected strength of 38,000 was based on a rough estimate of 1 soldier-policeman per 450 German residents, a ratio that would deploy 2.2 troopers per 1000 residents.

Actual deployment numbers were lower than the planning estimates. The total one year after the German surrender of 299,264 was slightly **higher than both the planned police- and army-type occupation final figures, but was soon reduced within a year to 117,224, a figure that remained** constant for the remainder of the occupation. The actual maximum Constabulary strength of 33,076 provided a ratio of 1.74 troopers per 1000 of population.

Originally, the occupation forces in Austria were counted separately, but were later added to the total for the entire occupation. The initial army-type occupation planning estimate for Austria of 73,000 troops equated to a high ratio of 56 soldiers per 1000 of population. However, the original **planning figures were based more on geographic area than population, as** the area soldier density ratio of 11.77 is similar to the army-type area density estimate of 8.87 for Germany.

The initial uncertainty about the size of the US occupation zone in Austria, part of which was later added to the French sector, and the mountainous terrain of some of the territory may account for the initial, higher planning estimates. In any event, actual deployment numbers were much smaller and within two years, there were only 11,345 US forces in Austria or **8.74 soldiers per 1000 of population. This lower, actual figure provided** 54 soldiers per square mile. See table 3 for the projected versus actual troop densities for the US occupation of Germany and Austria.

Indigenous support to the occupation forces only became a factor in the later stages of the occupation. Initially, occupation forces counted on no local support; however, as the occupation continued, indigenous forces were capable of providing support, allowing occupation forces to redeploy or to assist in the reconstruction of the new democratic Germany.

Postwar Japan

Situational Narrative

In contrast to the situation in Germany, at the time of the Japanese surrender in August 1945, the enemy government and armed forces remained largely intact. The surrender occurred suddenly as an immediate result of the atomic bombings of Hiroshima and Nagasaki and the Soviet invasion of Manchuria. The United States had been assembling forces for a projected two-phase invasion of the Japanese home islands. These assembled forces formed the initial basis of the occupation force.

By October 1945, 15 divisions, 7 corps, and 2 army headquarters had deployed to Japan.[52] These units were spread across the three major islands and the 46 political subdivisions referred to as prefectures. In the initial stages, multiple divisions were concentrated in urban settings, while in rural areas, divisions had responsibility for much larger areas often containing multiple prefectures.[53] This initial occupation force was almost immediately downsized to a more permanent force of four American divisions under one army and two corps headquarters, and a division equivalent of British Commonwealth troops who started arriving in February 1946.[54]

Despite the Commonwealth presence and unlike Germany, the Allied powers did not divide Japan into zones. The occupation was firmly under the control of American General of the Army Douglas MacArthur, the Supreme Commander for the Allied Powers, who governed Japan through the existing government structures. One of the primary goals of the occupation was the democratization of the government while removing the vestiges of unbridled militarism.[55]

In addition to occupying Japan, the US and Allied forces were responsible for securing the overseas territories occupied by Japanese forces and demobilizing the Japanese armed forces. The latter was a challenging task as there were over six million Japanese servicemen in uniform at the time of the surrender. Overseas, soldiers and Japanese civilians totaled six million, and all required repatriation. This mission was completed swiftly and by the end of 1945, all 4.3 million Japanese armed forces personnel in the home islands had been demobilized and all but 700,000 overseas personnel had been repatriated.[56]

The occupation force soon stabilized as a force of four American divisions and the division-size British Commonwealth Occupation Force (BCOF). While this structure continued through 1947 and 1948, the Commonwealth forces began downsizing as early as February 1947, with BCOF strength below 16,000 by the end of that year. The BCOF area of responsibility was adjusted accordingly. Though the US force structure remained intact, most of the divisions were somewhat skeletonized.[57]

By late 1948 MacArthur and his staff felt most of the goals of the occupation had been accomplished and executive policy officially sought to shift responsibility from the military government to Japanese civil authorities as soon as possible. As tensions in the region increased resulting from the communist victory in China, the orientation of the occupation forces shifted to tactical training. The outbreak of war in Korea in June 1950 effectively ended the occupation, although the official end would not come until the 1952 signing of the Peace Treaty of San Francisco.

Geographical Area, Terrain, and Population Density

Excluding Okinawa, which was occupied separately and ultimately converted into a US forward military base, the Japanese islands consisted of a total area of 142,859.73 square miles. The population in 1945 was 72.147 million, providing a national population density of 505 inhabitants per square mile.[58] The Japanese archipelago consists of four main islands referred to as the home islands. From north to south, the islands of Hokkaido, Honshu, Shikoku, and Kyushu extend 1300 miles from end to end. The island of Honshu takes up over 60 percent of the land mass and is 808 miles in length and 143 miles across at its widest point. Three-fourths of Japan's major cities including Tokyo, Yokohama, Osaka, Kyoto, Hiroshima, and Sendai are on the island of Honshu. The Japanese population is not distributed evenly across the home islands, largely because 73 percent of the land area is mountainous and, accordingly, far less settled. In 1945 therefore, most of the population was located in the less rugged coastal regions.[59]

Troop Deployment and Organization

Original planning estimates for the number of troops needed to occupy Japan called for a total of 600,000 soldiers, 315,000 American forces and contingents from China, the Soviet Union, and the British Commonwealth. These planning estimates were soon reduced to 340,000, of which 145,000 would be American forces.[60] As late as August 1945, MacArthur estimated a force of 500,000 would be required initially but he projected that number could be reduced to 200,000 within six months.[61]

Despite these planning estimates, the occupation force reached its peak strength in December 1945 with 354,675 forces deployed. However, demobilization and downsizing rapidly continued in early 1946. Despite the deployment of 40,236 British Commonwealth troops, total occupation force strength in August 1946 was roughly 192,236. Figure 6 illustrates how US forces were arrayed in Japan in August 1946.

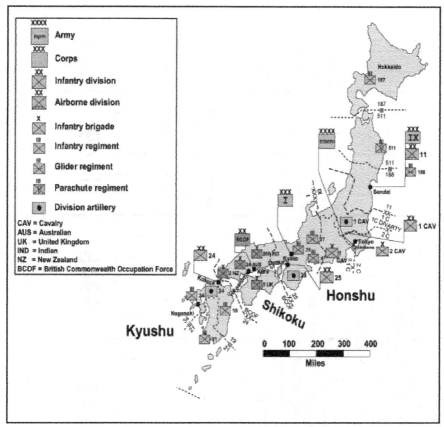

Figure 6. US troop deployment in Japan, August 1946.

After August 1946 the occupation force stabilized as the units that would remain in the islands were identified. However, the American divisions lost roughly one-third of their authorized strength, while the Commonwealth forces were also reduced, resulting in total strength numbers in June 1948 of 132,828.[62] This was approximately the troop strength in June 1950 when the start of the Korean War resulted in the deployment of all the major units in Japan to the Korean peninsula. Because the local government and police were still functioning, the American forces did not set up a new national, geographically based, military government structure as in Germany. Instead, divisions and regiments were stationed in the major cities in each prefecture, usually at former Japanese military installations.

Initially, the standard chain of echeloned headquarters was retained from division to corps to army to theater command. For most of the

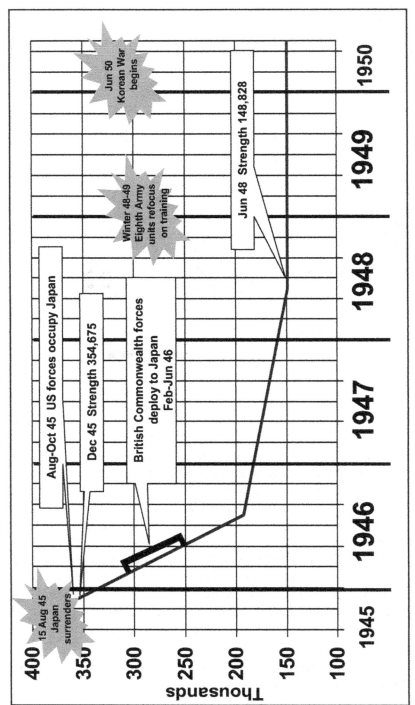

Figure 7. US troop strength during the occupation of Japan.

occupation, the Army retained two corps headquarters, one controlling the forces in the south, the other in the north. Early in 1950 on the eve of the Korean War, both corps headquarters were inactivated and almost immediately reactivated for deployment to Korea.

At the local level, the division was the basic occupation unit. Each subordinate element within the division was typically responsible for several prefectures based on population density. Then each of the subordinate regiments and the division artillery command delegated area responsibility to their subordinate battalions. This force structure continued even as units were downsized, when most regiments lost their third battalion and most division artilleries lost two or three firing batteries. As in the occupation of Germany, the rapid demobilization at the end of the war and the implementation of a peacetime individual replacement system resulted in the high turnover of personnel in most units. See figure 7 for the US troop strength during the occupation of Japan.

Indigenous Support

While the Japanese armed forces were quickly disbanded at the beginning of the occupation, the civil police force of 94,000 was allowed to remain intact and would continue at that level throughout the occupation period, although it was organizationally decentralized to the local level. No Japanese armed forces were raised during the occupation.[63]

Conclusion

The police-type occupation eventually implemented in Germany took its cue from the occupation of Japan. However, initial troop projections for Germany were slightly higher proportionally than projections for Japan. In terms of actual numbers deployed, the size of the force for the occupation of Germany was proportionally greater than the size of the force for the occupation of Japan, even if the Japanese police are included in occupation figures. The size of the Constabulary in Germany, as planned and executed, was also proportionally greater than the size of the existing Japanese police.

When considering the population of Japan, the occupation there was the largest ever executed by the military forces of the United States and the largest such operation analyzed in this work. However, despite the large Japanese population, the troop density was proportionally the lowest of any of the operations examined. Table 4 contains the population, area, and density information for the occupation of Japan.

Table 4. Troop Density in the Occupation of Japan

	Military Forces (ground forces)	Population	Area (square miles)	Population Density (per square mile)	Soldier Density		
					Per Area (soldiers per square mile)	Per Population (1 soldier per x residents) x=	Soldier Per 1000 Residents
Japan Occupation		72,147,000	142,859.73	505.01			
Projected (maximum size)	600,000				4.20	120.25	8.32
Occupation actual size maximum (Dec 45)	354,675				2.48	203.42	4.92
Occupation size (Aug 46)	192,236				1.35	375.30	2.66
British Commonwealth Forces (Aug 46)	40,236	20,000,000	22,000	909.01	1.83	497.07	2.01
Japanese police	94,000	72,147,000	142,859.73	505.01	0.66	767.52	1.30

The Malayan Emergency, 1948-60

Situational Narrative

Between 1948 and 1960, British and Commonwealth forces fought an extended, successful campaign against communist insurgents in the former colony of Malaya, which, in 1957 in the middle of hostilities, gained its independence. The Malay Peninsula is located at the southern extremity of the Southeast Asian mainland. Its strategic maritime position between India and China and its proximity to the Dutch East Indies (now Indonesia) had become of British colonial interest late in the 18th century. In addition to its strategic importance, the peninsula's natural resources made it a major supplier of tin and rubber.

Before the beginning of British interest in the area, Malaya had been divided into a number of smaller states. Throughout the 1800s, British influence grew, built upon the establishment of the trading city of Singapore on an island at the southern end of the Malay Peninsula in 1819. Singapore quickly prospered, and in 1867 that port as well as Malacca and Penang, two small port enclaves on the western Malay coast, formally became the British colony of the Straits Settlements. Between 1874 and 1914, the independent Malay states north of the British colony developed into a federation of states under a loose British protectorate known as the Malayan Union. In the 1930s the British began initiatives to unite the Malayan Union and the Straits Settlement, excluding Singapore, into one state with the intent of eventual independence. Internal Malayan politics and World War II delayed this process.[64]

In late 1941, during the early days of the war in the Pacific, a Japanese force of about 30,000, moving on foot and on bicycles, invaded and occupied Malaya in a rapid, 10-week campaign, forcing the surrender of over 100,000 British and Commonwealth troops at Singapore. This marked the greatest British military defeat of World War II. The Japanese occupied Malaya and Singapore until the end of the war in mid-1945.

After the Japanese surrender, the larger of two former anti-Japanese guerilla forces, the Communist Malayan Peoples' Anti-Japanese Army (MPAJA) attempted to fill the government void and, with its 10,000-man army, take control of Malaya. However, a force of 100,000 British Commonwealth troops, originally earmarked to retake southern Burma and Malaya from the Japanese, moved in and soon restored the prewar colonial government structure. Most of the guerilla forces, which had been largely ineffective against the Japanese because they had spent the war years primarily fighting among themselves, were demobilized after the British retook control of the peninsula. British administrators moved quickly to unify Malaya and establish the Malayan Federation under a British governor on 1 February 1948, despite Malay resentment of the Federation government that took powers away from the rulers of the local states. In the postwar era, the British, primarily for reasons of economy, sought to grant independence to most of their colonies. However, in Malaya, the growing communist threat among the Chinese segment of the Malayan population delayed this until the security threat could be eliminated or substantially reduced.

Though for the most part demobilized immediately after the war, the communist guerillas were quickly back in action, this time opposing the British and British-supported Malayan government. The Malayan communists were primarily ethnic Chinese, and soon gained support among the large Chinese portion of the Malayan population because of fears of ethnic Malay domination in the new federation. Additionally, Soviet support spurred the Malayan communists into action in early 1948, coinciding with communist initiatives in Berlin, Italy, and Greece and the pending communist victory in China.

Initial acts of violence soon escalated to the point that, in June 1948, the Federation government declared a state of emergency. This condition would continue until July 1960, three years after Malaya gained complete independence. The former MPAJA initially renamed itself the Malayan Peoples' Anti-British Army (MPABA), and then, in 1949 as the Malayan Races' Liberation Army (MRLA). The Commonwealth forces knew their enemy simply as the communist terrorists. The insurgent forces fluctuated in strength between 3000 and 10,000, generally averaging about 6000, until the success of counterinsurgency operations reduced their forces to less than 1000.[65]

The Malayan campaign can be divided into three general phases, an initial, disorganized phase (1948-50), a middle phase (1950-57) in which the British forces systematically destroyed the insurgency, and a final, mopping-up phase (1957-60).

In the initial phase from approximately June 1948 to June 1950, the British, expecting swift success and underestimating the insurgency, executed a disorganized, nonsystematic approach to their counterinsurgency operations, depending primarily on large-scale sweep operations executed by multiple battalions. However, such ponderous operations too often allowed the enemy to merely slip away and reappear elsewhere.[66] In spite of this, early triumphs over an equally disorganized insurgency fed the British expectations for a short campaign.[67] Initial British success resulted from the availability of a relatively large force in Malaya, after British withdrawals from India and Burma caused a reshuffling of their forces in Asia. Early successes included a July 1948 raid that killed the communist military leader, Lau Yew, and a September 1948 sweep through Johore province that destroyed 12 insurgent camps.[68]

Nevertheless, late in 1948, after a minor terror campaign against Europeans and Malays working in the rubber and tin industries, the MRLA withdrew to regroup and retrain. When the insurgents reemerged in force towards the end of 1949, they were operating in smaller, more self-contained groups. Renewed insurgent offensive operations began in Pahang province and spread throughout the country including attacks on rubber plantations, tin mines, railroads, convoys, and police and government officials. Counterinsurgency forces could not respond fast enough to prevent the attackers from melting away into the jungle wilderness. Instead of destroying insurgent forces, operations in this phase were merely driving them into the jungle.[69]

The middle phase (1950-57), when the counterinsurgency effort transformed into a highly successful, systematic approach, arose from the situation at the end of the initial phase. In early 1950 the insurgents seemed to be gaining the upper hand. The number of insurgent-led incidents increased in February by 80 percent, and continued to increase over the next eight months, demonstrating a higher level of coordination than ever before. At this point, the British command realized something had to change. While continued pressure on the insurgents had forced the MRLA to operate in smaller units, operations on both sides were resulting in almost equal casualties, a situation obviously unacceptable to the British.[70]

In response to this crisis, the senior British official in Malaya, High Commissioner Sir Henry Gurney, established the new post of Director of Operations. In 1950 the British government appointed retired Lieutenant General Sir Harold Briggs, an officer with extensive Asian experience, to the post. After assessing the situation, Briggs adopted a methodology, referred to as the "Briggs plan," that outlined the general counterinsurgency blueprint and would ultimately bring success to the British and Commonwealth forces.

In essence, the Briggs plan was a systematic approach designed to provide security for the rural population while simultaneously removing the primary sources of MRLA supply, food, and recruitment. Security forces would concentrate on completely removing the insurgent threat from a specific geographical region then move on to the next region. Briggs persuaded Gurney to set up coordinating committees comprised of representatives from all civil and military agencies involved in the campaign to formulate a coordinated response to the terrorists. Civil and military authorities would work in tandem and with complete coordination at all levels. A systematic approach to intelligence gathering was similarly adopted, with the civil police agencies and military intelligence agency taking the lead and working closely together.

The first major policy implemented as part of the Briggs plan was the resettlement of 500,000 Chinese squatters into more secure areas and settlements called New Villages. Gurney had already started resettling the squatters, but Briggs systemized and accelerated the process. The insurgents had long depended on the passive support of the squatters for supplies and recruits, using both persuasion and coercion. Resettlement proved to be a successful attempt to split this segment of the population from the insurgents. The New Villages provided proper sanitation, housing, schools, and hospitals, as well as security from insurgent encroachment. This resettlement project alone took until the end of 1952 to complete.[71] Another key element of the Briggs plan, designed to work in tandem with the resettlement, was Operation STARVATION, a comprehensive program implementing strict controls on food distribution to prevent the smuggling of foodstuffs to the insurgents. Food control operations were initially conducted in phases and decentralized in coordination with military operations, but were eventually centralized and executed countrywide.[72]

Operationally, instead of the haphazard assignment of missions and areas of operation seen in the past, beginning in July 1950, Briggs implemented a program of clearing Malaya state by state from south to north, designating each state in turn as a "priority area." Eventually, areas freed of insurgent activity would be designated "white areas," and all emergency restrictions would be removed.[73]

The Briggs plan took over three years to implement and encountered several obstacles along the way. At one point in late 1950, Briggs believed the situation had so deteriorated he flew to London to plead his case directly with the prime minister. It would take the arrival of a new High Commissioner for Malaya to maximize the effectiveness of the Briggs plan. Nevertheless, once a systematic, coordinated approach was implemented, providing security for the populace while at the same time concentrating on insurgent strongholds one at a time, the insurgency soon declined.[74]

After Gurney's death in a non-targeted MRLA ambush in October 1951, followed by Briggs' retirement for health reasons a month later, their posts were consolidated in February 1952 when the new Conservative Party government under Winston Churchill appointed General

Sir Gerald Templer as the new High Commissioner, Federation of Malaya.[75] After the setback caused by this personnel turbulence at the top of the British command, Templer reinvigorated the Briggs plan, adding more energy to its implementation through the unified, coordinated command structure his appointment created. For the first time, this new leadership unified military and civil functions of the counterinsurgency operation under one commander. Even more so than Briggs, Templer emphasized winning the support of all ethnic groups among the population of Malaya, with projected independence as the major incentive.[76] He continued Briggs' systematic approach to combat operations, but modified the original south-north axis approach after the southern state of Johore proved to be a difficult first step to take.

The MRLA was firmly entrenched in Johore and progress there was slow. In fact, Johore would not ultimately be cleared until 1958. Accordingly, a new approach was adopted which designated priority areas designed to divide areas of active insurgency in half. Once divided, a combat division would be concentrated each in the northern and southern sections to clear the now isolated insurgent strongholds. The first white area was declared in Malacca in September 1953, followed by four more areas over the next year and a half. By April 1955 the insurgent area had been successfully divided into two smaller sections, further degrading the communists' ability to coordinate their operations. This insurgent partition would be solidified in August 1957 when most of the state of Selangor would be declared white.[77]

As early as May 1954, when Templer departed Malaya, it was clear the British and Commonwealth forces had defeated the insurgency and Malaya was ready for self-government.[78] However, the insurgents remained a dangerous force and Templer strongly recommended the continuation of the emergency status in Malaya until the communist threat was totally eliminated.[79] In July 1955 the Malayan people held their first nationwide general elections and the chief minister selected from the electoral results, Tunku Abdul Rahman, soon sought surrender from the MRLA through peace talks. However, these talks ended in failure in December 1955 and the insurgency continued.

By the time Malaya gained independence in 1957 and Rahman became the country's first prime minister, over 60 percent of the national area had been cleared of active insurgents. In the final phase of the Emergency, from 1957 to July 1960, British, Commonwealth, and Malayan forces concentrated on the two insurgent strongholds, first in the south in Johore and then in the north near the Thai border. Former insurgents surrendered en masse, while terrorist incidents and contacts were reduced to only a handful by

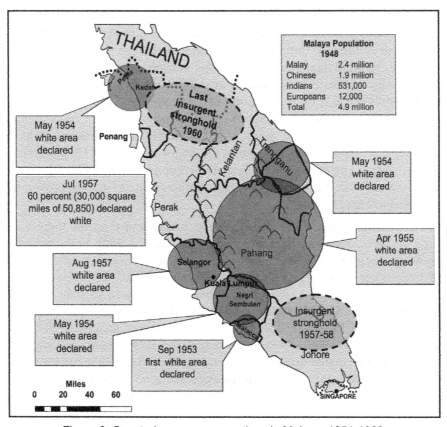

Figure 8. Counterinsurgency operations in Malaya, 1951-1960.

1959. The last major operations in the southern states of Johore and Perak ended in mid-1958, leaving a cadre of about 1000 MRLA stalwarts in the north near the Thai border. Cooperation and coordinated operations with the Thais cut this force in half by 1960 and on 31 July 1960, the new **Malay government officially declared the Emergency over, retaining only** emergency restrictions in a few isolated areas along the Thai border. An MRLA remnant of approximately 500 insurgents took refuge across the Thai border, awaiting better conditions to return to Malaya, effectively ending the insurgency.[80] Figure 8 illustrates the British and Commonwealth forces counterinsurgency operations in Malaya.

Geographical Area, Terrain, and Population Density

Malaya extends 500 miles from the border with Thailand to the island-city of Singapore. At its maximum width, the peninsula is 200 miles wide. The insurgency was nationwide, consuming the entire 50,850 square miles of Malaya, an expanse of slightly less than half the size of Italy. The mountain range in the center of the peninsula reaches 7000 feet in elevation and is covered by thick jungle. Numerous streams and rivers flow east and west from the mountains. Away from the mountains, most of the rest of Malaya consists of a lush, trackless, evergreen rain forest and undergrowth. The jungle consumes four-fifths of the area of Malaya, and the remaining one-fifth is the area along the southern and western coasts, where during the time of the Malayan Emergency, the majority of the population lived.[81]

The Malay people are the original population on the peninsula. Economic prosperity in the 19th and 20th centuries brought thousands of foreign laborers and settlers to Malaya, resulting in the establishment of large ethnic Chinese and Indian communities within the Malayan population. In fact, by 1948 the Chinese population in Malaya was 1.9 million, while the Malay population was only slightly larger at 2.4 million.[82] This sizeable Chinese population included the more than 500,000 squatters who lived and farmed land to which they had no title along the edge of the jungle. The communist insurgency in Malaya during the Emergency worked among and recruited almost exclusively from the Malayo-Chinese population. The squatters provided a fertile population base from which the insurgents could draw and given their remote locations, a security problem for the counterinsurgency forces who had to defend those areas.

Combining all ethnic groups, Malaya had an estimated population of 4,856,000 in 1948.[83] Given the land area of Malaya and the extensive size of the jungle areas, the relative population density of 95.49 inhabitants per square mile may be somewhat misleading since large areas were virtually uninhabited. However, because the insurgents worked among the populace and moved around the entire country, this relative figure will be used here for comparative purposes.

British Troop Deployment and Organization

For the Malayan Emergency, the British government initially deployed a force of 16 infantry and armored car battalions and later a maximum of 30 battalions. Once the full force was assembled in early 1952, its size, in spite of unit rotations, remained roughly between 26 and 28 battalions until late 1956 after which the deployed force was gradually downsized to 21 battalions by the end of the Emergency. Including a force of about 5000 support troops, the peak British and Commonwealth strength was about 30,000. At any given time, three deployed battalions could be expected to be refitting or retraining in rest areas in Singapore, while the rest would be conducting counterinsurgency operations.[84]

The British force package in Malaya consisted of three major components: a group of British Army battalions, which rotated in and out of Malaya during the Emergency, a large force of Gurkha infantry battalions deployed for the duration of the conflict, and battalions and smaller units from the British Commonwealth, including Malaya. The non-Malayan units rotated in a manner similar to the British battalions.

The British infantry battalions and supporting units formed part of the regular establishment. However, as the British had adopted its first-ever peacetime conscription, or "National Service," in 1948, many of the soldiers and officers of these units were non-regular National Servicemen. The maximum term of service for National Servicemen was two years.[85] By 1951, with the deployment for the Emergency in full swing, British and non-Malayan Commonwealth units deployed for tours of approximately three years. For the British units, this meant, given the short periods of service for the National Servicemen who made up to 60 percent of the enlisted strength of the infantry battalions, and the longer three-year troop rotations of the battalions in which they served, these battalions had to endure internal turnover during their tours in Malaya.[86]

Early on, the British deployed an elite force of three Guards infantry battalions under the command of the 2d Guards Brigade. However, these battalions, after serving tours of less than two years, were replaced by regular infantry units that did not have ceremonial duties in Britain. In addition to infantry and armored car units, the British employed a battalion-size special operations unit, the 22d Special Air Service (SAS) Regiment. The SAS, a former World War II-era unit was reconstituted in Malaya from a combination of smaller special operations units and a British Territorial Army (i.e., reserve component) unit made up of war veterans of the original SAS. After Malaya, the British would retain the SAS as their elite counterterrorism, special operations unit.[87]

While the British rotated their own regular units of conscripts through Malaya, they also employed the only remaining portion of the former British Indian Army still serving the Crown: eight battalions of a combination of Gurkha enlisted men and British and Gurkha officers. The Gurkhas are descendents of fierce tribal warriors from Nepal, the mountainous kingdom situated between India and China. In the days of British rule in India, Gurkhas formed a large component of the British-run Indian Army. During World War II, there were 40 Gurkha battalions, totaling 112,000 soldiers. After Indian independence in 1947, an agreement with the Kingdom of Nepal divided the Gurkhas between the new Indian Army and the British Army. The Indians retained six regiments of two or more battalions each, and the British incorporated eight battalions in four regiments directly into their army for the first time.[88]

The redistribution of Gurkha forces was effective 1 January 1948 and the British Gurkha units were stationed in Malaya, Singapore, and Hong Kong when the Malayan Emergency began. For the most part, all eight Gurkha battalions spent the majority of the next 12 years in Malaya conducting counterinsurgency operations, although two battalions later garrisoned other posts in the Far East. Gurkha soldiers served initial four-year enlistments, although most stayed for standard 15-year careers.[89] Therefore, the Gurkha units in Malaya ultimately provided a large part of the continuity and stability in the British forces stationed there. The generally superior efficiency of Gurkha units in counterinsurgency operations was clearly indicated in statistical analyses maintained by the British command.[90] The British command formed larger Gurkha headquarters units, including a division headquarters and four brigade headquarters. These units usually controlled other units, not just Gurkha battalions.

The Commonwealth contingent included battalion-size elements from East Africa, Fiji, Australia, and New Zealand. These units, like the British battalions, rotated through Malaya for tours of one to three and a half years. The British chain of command considered the Fiji battalion to be the best unit to participate in the Emergency, followed closely by the East African units.[91] In addition to these overseas nations, Commonwealth forces included an expanding force of Malay soldiers.

The Malay Regiment, a force recruited only from men of Malay ethnic background, had been formed before World War II but was destroyed in the 1941-42 Singapore campaign. After the war, the regiment was rebuilt with two battalions. In 1948 a third battalion was formed. Starting in 1952, another four battalions were formed in succession. All seven would be committed to counterinsurgency operations. In preparation for Malayan independence, the British authorities formed a new organization, the Federation (of Malaya) Regiment, which did not have the ethnic restrictions of the Malay regiment.

Despite the inclusion of the other ethnic groups in Malaya into the new regiment, recruiting was slow and only one battalion had been raised by late 1953. Nevertheless, once this battalion deployed, it marked a significant event in the Malayan Emergency. For the first time, Malayan battalions formed the majority of the units engaged in counterinsurgency operations. After Malayan independence in 1957, the battalions of the Malay and Federation regiments would form the backbone of the nation's new military forces.[92] See figure 9 for a time line of force deployments in Malaya.

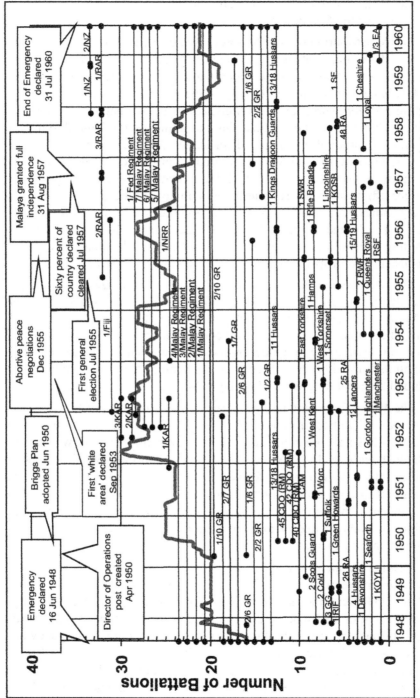

Figure 9. British, Commonwealth, and indigenous forces in the Malayan Emergency, 1948-1960.

Organizationally, the British command in Malaya was separated initially into a decentralized, colonial civil government and separate police and military functions. Eventually, a director of military operations was appointed to coordinate all operations against the insurgents using all available forces. However, civil government remained separate until, under Templer, a completely unified command was adopted.[93]

Initially, the counterinsurgency effort was divided into three area commands called subdistricts.[94] However, as troop strength grew, a more conventional division/brigade structure was adopted. In its mature structure, the British and Commonwealth forces employed two division headquarters, the 16th Gurkha Division in the north and the 1st Federation Division in the south. Under these two divisions, there were up to eight brigade headquarters to control the battalions engaging the enemy.[95]

Paralleling the standard military chain of command and as a coordinating measure between civil, police, and military authorities, Briggs had formed war executive committees (WEC) at the state and district levels, which were responsible for all decisions and actions related to the Emergency in their respective districts and states. Later, members of Templer's staff regularly toured the WECs with the authority to make on-the-spot decisions in Templer's name.[96]

The British employed about one soldier for every two square miles of Malaya and 1 soldier for about every 162 inhabitants, equating to 6.17 soldiers per 1000 of population. Because operations against the insurgents were primarily focused in remote, sparsely populated areas, the geographic figure may well prove to be more significant than the demographic figure. Table 5 charts deployed troop density in relation to population and geographic area for the Malayan Emergency at maximum deployment.

Indigenous Support

From the start, the British depended on extensive indigenous support in their counterinsurgency effort. As mentioned above, eight regular battalions of army troops were organized from Malayan personnel. In addition to these soldiers, the British command also established large paramilitary and police forces. A new Malayan police force, initially 10,000 strong, was organized in August 1948. This force ultimately grew to 40,000. The large police force eventually freed military forces so that the latter could be massed to eradicate the guerillas in whole areas. However, while the police were less expensive to equip and train than units of soldiers, statistics collected by the British command showed that army forces had a comparatively better performance in counterinsurgency operations than

Table 5. Troop Density in the Malayan Emergency

	Military Forces (at maximum)	Population	Area (square miles)	Population Density (per square mile)	Soldier Density		
					Per Area (soldiers per square mile)	Per Population (1 soldier per x residents) x=	Soldiers Per 1000 Residents
Malaya 1948-60	30,000	4,856,000	50,850	95.49	0.59	161.87	6.18

the police did. This meant the police, while valuable for specific types of missions, were no substitute for soldiers in counterinsurgency operations.

To provide local self-defense, in 1949 the British formed a force of 30,000 Special Constables and 15,000 part-time village Home Guards. These forces would ultimately grow to 44,000 and 250,000 respectively. In particular, the police forces provided intelligence and participated in counterinsurgency operations. By 1952 a 4000-member federation police field force was operational. The Special Constabulary was organized to guard vital installations, plantations, and mines, and to enforce the food control operation. This force's became vital when the relocation of Chinese squatters forced the insurgents to turn to the mines and plantations for supplies. The Home Guards, sometimes called the Kampong Guards, were designed purely for local self-defense.[97]

The primary intelligence agency in Malaya was the federal police force's Special Branch. After a slow and disorganized start, under Templer this agency took the lead in gathering intelligence on the insurgents, and during the later stages of the Emergency, was a highly effective organization. They were particularly adept at gaining information from captured or surrendered insurgents and from locals in areas of insurgent activity. By 1954 most counterinsurgency operations were based directly on Special Branch intelligence, and Special Branch officers were attached directly to higher army headquarters. As Templer's policies began to take effect, the flow of information increased substantially.[98]

Templer increased the involvement of the local population in the fight against the guerrillas. He strengthened a preexisting, unarmed Chinese Home Guard force designed to defend the New Villages by arming them and increasing their size so that, by 1954, 150 New Villages were able to conduct their own defense. Additionally, he implemented a three-phase plan for the overall improvement of the Home Guard which ultimately resulted in that force taking over for the police in village self-defense, while even providing some offensive capability of its own. This latter element, the Operational Home Guard, functioned in areas where military or police forces were in short supply, and provided local expertise to military units conducting nearby operations. Templer also reorganized the Special Constabulary for offensive operations by forming them into an effective local patrol force called area security units.[99]

Conclusion

The British operated in Malaya with extensive indigenous support and executed counterinsurgency operations for 12 years, defeating the communist insurgency while granting Malaya independence. The period from 1952-54 was the most decisive for British operations in Malaya. It was at this time that a unified, systematic approach to counterinsurgency operations broke the back of the insurgency.

For military forces, at the maximum, the British employed an area troop density of 0.59 soldiers per square mile throughout the country and a population troop density of 6.18 soldiers for every 1000 Malayan inhabitants (or 1 soldier per every 161.9 inhabitants). While the insurgency existed nationwide, most counterinsurgency operations were conducted in remote, underpopulated areas, and, over time, indigenous forces became available to provide local security for the populated areas.

The Balkans: Bosnia and Kosovo

Bosnia

Situational narrative

With the dissolution of Yugoslavia in the early 1990s, most of the former, ethnically based states of that country became independent entities. However, the state of Bosnia-Herzegovina was a mixture of three ethnic groups: Catholic Croats, Moslem Bosnians, and Orthodox Serbs. These factions came to blows after a referendum in early 1992 resulted in a Bosnian declaration of independence. The Bosnian Serbs boycotted the referendum and then began an armed insurrection, with the goal of partitioning Bosnia along ethnic lines and annexing the Serbian area to neighboring Serbia. The three ethnic groups warred against each other from 1992 to 1995, supported by Serbia and to a lesser extent by Croatia. Serbia later merged with Serbian Montenegro to create a new Yugoslavia.[100]

In March 1994 the Bosnian Croats and Bosnian Moslem inhabitants joined forces to form the Federation of Bosnia and Herzegovina, in opposition to the Bosnian Serbs, who in turn formed their own state called *Republika Srpska* (*RS*). On 21 November 1995, in Dayton, Ohio, the warring parties initialed a peace agreement, which was implemented the following month. The Dayton Agreement (also known as the Dayton Accords) layered the Bosnian government so, at the highest level, there was a national government for external and fiscal affairs. At a secondary level, the two warring factions, which were about equal in geographic and demographic size, retained specific control over internal government functions in the areas they controlled.

As part of the Dayton Agreement, the UN appointed a new agency, the Office of the High Representative (OHR), to oversee the

Figure 10. The Balkans.

implementation of the civilian aspects of the agreement. Additionally, to implement and monitor the military aspects of the agreement, the UN established, under the auspices of NATO, an international peacekeeping force called the implementation force (IFOR). IFOR consisted of 60,000 troops that replaced a weaker, UN-sponsored force that had not included American participation. IFOR existed for a year and, in December 1996, a smaller, NATO-led stabilization force (SFOR) replaced IFOR. SFOR carried out the same mission begun by IFOR, continuing the deterrence of renewed hostilities. Planning estimates for SFOR troop strength was 30,000, roughly half the IFOR strength. However, this reduction in strength occurred only over time, as SFOR maintained a total strength of 32,000 as late as 1998. Initially, SFOR was to exist for 18 months. However, it remained operational until December 2004 when European Union peacekeeping forces (EUFOR) replaced it.

Throughout the SFOR deployment, units rotated in and out of Bosnia and the strength of the force gradually declined over time. For example, the American contingent, which had started with 8500 in 1996, was reduced to 3900 by February 1999 and to 1400 by December 2002. SFOR total strength was 18,000 in 2003. EUFOR was 7000 strong when it took over at the end of 2004.[101]

Throughout the mission, the peacekeepers strove to maintain security as the civilian government was reestablished and to demobilize the armed forces of the two warring factions as much as possible. By late 2004 all participating countries determined the mission of the IFOR/SFOR had been a success. These successes included the restoration of most infrastructure, general area stability, and employment opportunities. Additionally, the SFOR restored law and order and well-trained Bosnian police officers, not ethnically based police or military forces, assumed the responsibility for maintaining it.[102]

Geographical area, terrain, and population density

The area of Bosnia is 202.62 square miles. In 1995 the population was roughly four million, about 300,000 less than the previous census conducted before the civil wars.[103] Internally, Bosnia was divided into two territories, one controlled by the joint Bosnian Moslem-Croat Federation (about 51 percent of the country) and one controlled by the Bosnian Serb-led *RS* (about 49 percent of the country). Except for a small strip of coastline along the Adriatic Sea surrounded by Croatian territorial waters, Bosnia is mountainous and land locked, surrounded by Croatia in the north and west, the Yugoslavian republic of Serbia in the east, and the Yugoslavian republic of Montenegro in the south. Herzegovina is the designation generally given to the southern portion of Bosnian territory.

Troop deployment and organization

Both the IFOR and SFOR were organized around three multinational divisions, Multinational Division-North (MND-N) under a rotating American division headquarters staff, Multinational Division-Southwest (MND-SW) under British command, and Multinational Division-Southeast (MND-SE), under French command. While staffs from these three nations commanded the divisional sectors, units from various NATO countries and several non-NATO nations, such as the new Russian Federation, the Ukraine, Egypt, and Finland, also took part.[104] See figure 11.

The three division commands deployed subordinate brigade- and battalion-size forces into specific geographical sectors. Each division typically had three brigades during the IFOR period and deployed from 9 to

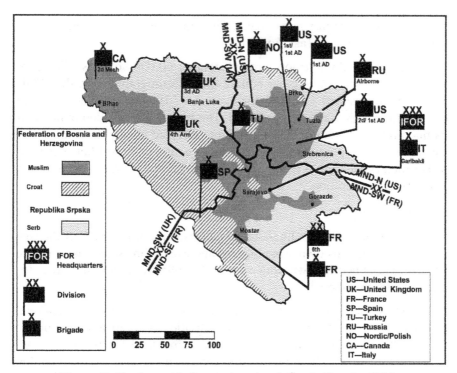

Figure 11. Deployment of peacekeeping forces in Bosnia, 1996.

11 infantry, tank, or reconnaissance battalions. During the SFOR period, these forces were reduced initially by half and then over time to about a quarter of the original force size.

In addition to these forces in the field, the IFOR headquarters in the Bosnian capital of Sarajevo retained a small mobile reaction force. For peacekeeping duties, the IFOR/SFOR established and operated from a series of base camps, a system repeated in Kosovo and Iraq in subsequent years. In Bosnia, one base camp was established for every 536.34 soldiers deployed in the US sector and one base for every 682.15 soldiers for just the US contingent. Base camp density is an important consideration in contingency operations. However, information concerning this subject is only readily available in the case of the Bosnia deployment. [105]

NATO organized the IFOR headquarters using the staff of a preexisting NATO command, the Allied Command, Europe, Rapid Reaction Corps, commanded in 1995 by a British lieutenant general. The major US command, US Army, Europe (USAREUR) (Forward), was located outside of Bosnia in Hungary and orchestrated both American support to the peacekeeping mission and the required logistic support, most of which operated out of Hungary and Croatia. The American force package in Bosnia was also known as Task Force Eagle.[106]

At its peak, IFOR troop strength totaled 60,000 soldiers. This provided about three soldiers per square mile. Demographically, the IFOR deployment provided 1 soldier for every 66.7 Bosnian residents, a ratio of 15 soldiers per 1000 of population. The reduced SFOR deployment, at its maximum of roughly 30,000 soldiers, provided about 149 soldiers per square mile and 1 soldier to 133.3 residents, a ratio of 7.5 soldiers per 1000 of Bosnian population. Figure 12 illustrates US and MND-N force levels in the Bosnia operation.[107]

Indigenous support

Initially in Bosnia, indigenous support was minimal. Each of the two warring sides had its own armed forces and each of the three major ethnic groups maintained its own police force. In 1995 these various forces totaled 45,000 members.[108]

In December 1995 the UN authorized a 1721-member international police task force (IPTF) to oversee the activities of the local ethnic police forces. Though it took almost eight months before the IPTF was operational, in the four years following its implementation, the force trained 16,000 Bosnian police officers. This, coupled with the establishment of stable local government, resulted in an increasingly effective role in local law enforcement. However, there was no nationwide law enforcement agency. The Dayton Agreement allowed the continued coexistence of ethnic police forces and as of 2005, Bosnian-Serb government officials continued to hinder efforts to create a nationwide police force.[109]

In addition to ethnic police forces, the warring factions fielded sizeable armed forces in 1995 when the Bosnian mission began. The Bosnian-Serb army, *Vojska Republike Srpske* (*VRS*) totaled 80,000 troops organized into six corps. The opposing Federation fielded its own Army of Bosnia and Herzegovina (VF), also about 80,000 strong with seven corps. The VF had distinct Bosnian-Croat and Bosnian-Moslem elements, representing the two groups in the Federation. Both armies downsized and the *VRS* lost most of its heavy equipment. By 2005 the two armed forces combined fielded 12,000 soldiers, with 8000 in the VF and 4000 in the *VRS*.[110]

Kosovo

Situational narrative

In addition to Bosnia, other areas of ethnic conflict existed in the former states of Yugoslavia in the late 1990s. Kosovo, a province in southern Serbia

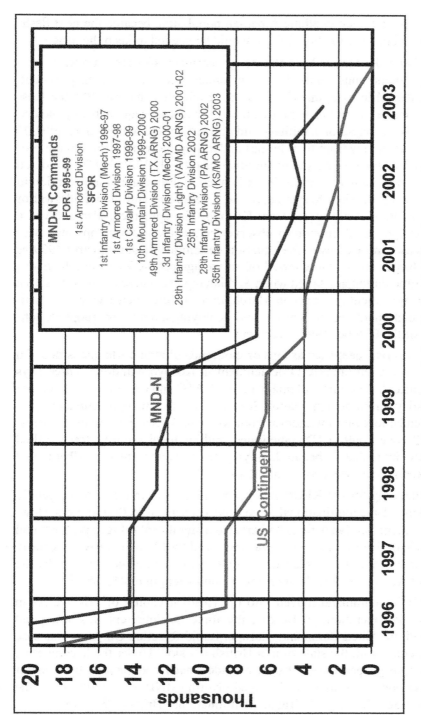

MND-N Commands
IFOR 1995-99
1st Armored Division
SFOR
1st Infantry Division (Mech) 1996-97
1st Armored Division 1997-98
1st Cavalry Division 1998-99
10th Mountain Division 1999-2000
49th Armored Division (TX ARNG) 2000
3d Infantry Division (Mech) 2000-01
29th Infantry Division (Light) (VA/MD ARNG) 2001-02
25th Infantry Division 2002
28th Infantry Division (PA ARNG) 2002
35th Infantry Division (KS/MO ARNG) 2003

Figure 12. Number of troops deployed to Bosnia, US sector.

51

with a predominantly ethnic Albanian population, became the next flash-point where a multinational force would be needed to keep the peace.

Under the former Yugoslavian government, Kosovo enjoyed a relatively autonomous status. However, under autocratic Serbian president, Slobodan Milosevic, this changed so significantly that by 1998 the Kosovar Albanians were in open revolt. Milosevic's subsequent heavy-handed response, using Serbian military and police forces to remove over 400,000 ethnic Albanians from their homes and killing more than 1500 in the process, escalated the crisis to the international level. While NATO pondered a military option, diplomacy initially averted international intervention in October 1998, when Serbia agreed to a cease-fire and the withdrawal of most of its security forces from Kosovo. The agreement also allowed a NATO-sponsored mission to observe the situation and compliance with the cease-fire. However, the situation deteriorated again in early 1999 as Serb forces initiated a renewed offensive against the Kosovar Albanians. This time diplomacy failed when Serbian representatives refused to sign a peace agreement in France in March, immediately intensifying their anti-Albanian operations in Kosovo and deploying even more troops in defiance of the October 1998 agreement.

The crisis deepened as tens of thousands of ethnic Albanians fled. On 20 March even the NATO detachment in Kosovo withdrew. Three days later, after last minute diplomacy failed, NATO and UN forces commenced a 77-day air campaign against Serbia. The air campaign ultimately persuaded Milosevic to withdraw from Kosovo. As Serbian forces withdrew on 12 June 1999, a UN-sanctioned multinational security force, called KFOR, immediately began deploying from staging areas in Albania and the Republic of Macedonia into Kosovo.[111]

Planning for the KFOR had been ongoing for months. As originally envisioned, the multinational force was to consist of 28,000 soldiers. However, recent Serbian actions had created a significant refugee problem and the size of the projected force was increased by 17,000 to provide security for the return of the displaced.[112] KFOR completed its deployment by the end of August 1999 with an on-the-ground strength of 41,618.[113]

KFOR command moved into the Kosovar capital of Priština. As in the initial operations in Bosnia, the force headquarters was structured around the Allied Command, Europe, Rapid Reaction Corps, in this case augmented with the staff from a British division. Under the headquarters were five geographically based brigades, each commanded by a major NATO power: Multinational Brigade-North (MNB-N) initially under the French 3d Mechanized Brigade, Multinational Brigade-West (MNB-W)

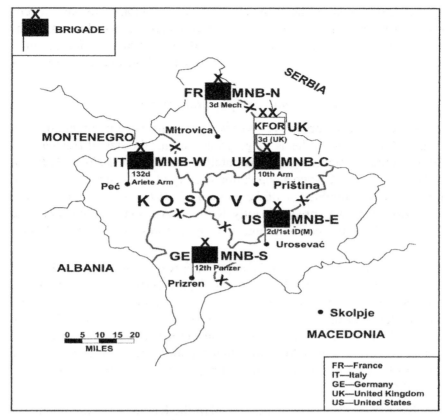

Figure 13. KFOR organization, 1999.

commanded by the staff of the Italian 132d "Ariete" Armored Brigade, Multinational Brigade-Center (MNB-C) under the British 10th Armoured Brigade, Multinational Brigade-South (MNB-S) staffed by the German 12th Panzer Brigade, and Multinational Brigade-East (MNB-E) under the US 2d Brigade, 1st Infantry Division (Mechanized). See figure 13. KFOR headquarters also maintained a small military police and maneuver force under its own control for special situations.[114.]

While the forces deployed to Kosovo rotated, the headquarters and **five-brigade structure was maintained. US forces on average rotated every** six months. After the 11 September 2001 attacks on the United States, mobilized Army National Guard headquarters and troops played an increased role in the US contribution to the KFOR, replacing several active Army units designated for operations in Iraq or elsewhere.[115]

Analysts consider the Kosovo operation to be the most successful operation of its kind in the post-Cold War era. This success has been marked by the disarmament of the Albanian Kosovo Liberation Army, strong economic growth and the implementation of local and regional elections within two years.[116] As of this writing (2005), the operation continues, though KFOR has been downsized to four brigades and an overall strength of 17,000.[117]

Geographical area, terrain, and population density

Kosovo is a region of five river valleys surrounded by mountains. Its area of 4204 square miles is roughly one-quarter the size of Bosnia. The 1999 population figure of approximately 1.9 million was almost half that of Bosnia, giving Kosovo a population density of 469 residents per square mile, more than double that of the previous Balkan peacekeeping mission. The population was predominantly Kosovar Albanian (88 percent), the majority of whom became refugees in the months preceding the NATO intervention.

Most of the remainder of the population was ethnically Serb. Despite its current predominant Albanian ethnicity, the Serbs consider Kosovo an integral part of Serbia because it was the heartland of medieval Serbia and the location of a significant Serbian defeat at the hands of the Ottoman Turks in 1389. In 1999 over half of the Kosovar population lived in towns or villages; only five cities had a population of over 50,000, the largest of which is the capital of Priština, with a population of more than 500,000.[118]

The Kosovo war prior to the arrival of the KFOR was a nightmare for the Kosovar population. About 863,000 ethnic Albanians had fled Kosovo for refuge in neighboring Macedonia, Albania, and as far away as Bosnia. Another several hundred thousand were displaced within Kosovo. Upon the departure of the Serbian security forces and before the arrival of the KFOR, roughly half of the 137,900 ethnic Serb population had fled to Serbia proper, Montenegro, and Macedonia. Other Serbs within Kosovo fled to ethnic Serbian enclaves, most of which were near the boundary with the rest of Serbia.[119]

Geographically, Kosovo is located in the extreme southwest of Serbia with the mountainous Republic of Montenegro (at times joined in federation with Serbia) to the northwest, Albania to the southwest, and Slavic Macedonia, an independent state formerly part of Yugoslavia, to the south. The Montenegrins speak a dialect of Serbian, while the Macedonians speak a Slavic language closer to Bulgarian than to Serbian. The predominantly Moslem Albanians, both in Albania and Kosovo, speak a non-Slavic language not directly related to Serbian or Macedonian. While

54

the Serbs are predominantly Orthodox Christians in religious heritage, the ethnic Albanians in Kosovo are predominantly Islamic, a relic of the several centuries of occupation of the region by the Ottoman Turks in late medieval and early modern times.

Troop deployment and organization

As previously cited, the Kosovo operational element, KFOR, deployed a maximum force of 41,618 soldiers organized into a headquarters element and five brigades. Each brigade was assigned a sector of responsibility that provided approximately a brigade of peacekeepers for every 394,000 inhabitants. In terms of population, the KFOR maximum troop strength provided over 21 soldiers per 1000 of population and 88 soldiers per square mile of the relatively compact Kosovo region. Fearing KFOR would be required to combat the Serbian security forces and provide security for the return of refugees, this comparatively large force was deployed to the region.

Contingents from 38 NATO and non-NATO nations were represented in the KFOR organization, with the command rotating among the most prominently represented nations. The initial large size of the force was somewhat tempered by the short, six-month rotation periods. For example, between 1999 and 2005, the US contingent alone had 13 commanders. Other contingents were similar. Even KFOR commanders rotated frequently as different countries assumed the KFOR command. In 2001 the tour of duty for the KFOR commander was extended to one year.[120] The lack of continuity in KFOR did not seem to have any direct affect on its operational capabilities. By 2002 some US units were even returning to Kosovo for a second tour of duty. KFOR was reduced in size over time to 32,000 by the end of 2001, 30,000 in 2002, and to 17,000 by 2005.[121]

Even while the KFOR troop reductions were beginning, trouble flared up in the city of Mitrovica in the French sector. Mitrovica became the focus of ethnic clashes throughout the KFOR operation, as extremists on both sides rallied to the city. This flashpoint required frequent reinforcement, as British, German, and American forces aided the French, resulting in a regular rotation of forces from other sectors to this particularly hot spot.[122]

Indigenous support

In June 1999 when KFOR became operational, there was no available indigenous support in Kosovo. Serbian civil administrators, who had exclusively held all such positions for a decade, had fled. Police and military forces in Kosovo in June 1999 were all Serbian and were ordered to leave the country as part of the cease-fire agreement. The ethnic Albanian Kosovo Liberation Army (KLA) attempted to fill the void, but was part of the problem and not an element capable of providing support to KFOR; the KLA was disarmed by September 1999.[123]

In early 2000 NATO authorities transformed the former KLA into a new civil defense/emergency management organization, the Kosovo Protection Corps (KPC) or in Albanian, *Trupat Mbrojtëse Të Kosovës* (*TMK*). The KPC strength initially was 5052, recruited primarily from the 20,000 former members of the KLA.[124]

While the KPC provided civic support, KFOR initially had sole law enforcement responsibility. An international police force, under the auspices of the UN mission in Kosovo (UNMIK) was formed, eventually reaching a total strength of 4450 by the end of 2000.[125] Also in 2000, UNMIK formed a local police force, the Kosovo Police Service (KPS), which started with 842 officers and expanded to a size of 4933 by September 2002.[126]

Balkans Conclusion

The two peacekeeping missions in the Balkans share certain characteristics. The concept of multinational place-keeper organizations where a unit has responsibility for a specific, geographical area of responsibility and through which a series of units rotate over time was developed in Bosnia and applied on a smaller scale in Kosovo. In both cases, indigenous support was practically nonexistent at the beginning of the mission, requiring the deployment of large forces in proportion to the population and area. In Bosnia NATO deployed a maximum area troop density of three soldiers per square mile, while in the more compact Kosovo, there were 10 soldiers per square mile. Clearly, however, the deployment size of the force was determined based primarily on demographics rather than geography. The force deployed to Bosnia at its maximum had a population troop density of 15 soldiers for every 1000 inhabitants (or 1 soldier for every 67 inhabitants). The ratio in Kosovo, with a population density almost two and a half times higher than that of Bosnia, was 21.13 soldiers per 1000 residents (or 48 residents per soldier). Table 6 displays the density statistics for the Balkans' deployments.

Table 6. Troop Density in the Balkans Operations

	Military Forces (at maximum)	Population	Area (square miles)	Population Density (per square mile)	Soldier Density		
					Per Area (soldiers per square mile)	Per Population (1 soldier per x residents) x=	Soldiers Per 1000 Residents
Bosnia		4,000,000	19,741.00	202.62			
IFOR 1995-96	60,000				3.00	66.67	15.00
SFOR planned 1996-99	30,000				1.52	133.33	7.50
Kosovo 1999		1,970,000	4203.60	468.64			
	41,618				9.90	47.34	21.13

Notes

1. Congress did not ratify the treaty until 11 April 1899.

2. Louis Morton, *The Fall of the Philippines*. United States Army in World War II: The War in the Pacific, CMH Pub 5-2. (Washington, DC, US Army Center of Military History, 1953), 4-5.

3. *Correspondence Relating to the War with Spain including the Insurrection in the Philippine Islands and the China Relief Expedition, April 15, 1898 to July 30, 1902*. vol. 2 (Washington, DC: US Army Center of Military History, 1993), 1070, 1077, 1154-5; Brian Linn, *The Philippine War 1899-1902* (Lawrence, KS: University Press of Kansas, 2000), 198-9.

4. Linn, 215.

5. Morton, 5-6; Linn, 15.

6. Linn, 255, 277.

7. *Correspondence Relating to the War with Spain*, 1053. Only 13 regiments were ultimately raised.

8. Linn, 226.

9. *Correspondence Relating to the War with Spain*, 1217-8. Strength figures are based on a combination of Otis' and MacArthur's monthly returns and their reported sick rate (which was given as a percentage of total assigned strength.)

10. Linn, 255, 277.

11. *Correspondence Relating to the War with Spain*, 1275.

12. Stewart, 274.

13. Linn, 204, 210.

14. Harold Zink, *The United States in Germany, 1944-1955* (Princeton: Van Nostrand, 1957), 352; Oliver J. Frederiksen, *The American Military Occupation of Germany 1945-1953* (Darmstadt, Germany: Historical Division, Headquarters, US Army Europe, 1953), 121.

15. Earl F. Ziemke, *The U.S. Army in the Occupation of Germany 1944-1946*, Army Historical Series, CMH-Pub 30-6 (Washington, DC: US Army Center of Military History, 1970), 321.

16. Ziemke, 320; Frederiksen, 46.

17. Ziemke, 320, 339.

18. Frederiksen, 50; Office of the Chief Historian, European Command, "The First Year of the Occupation" in *Occupation Forces in Europe Series, 1945-1945*, vol.1 (Frankfurt, Germany: US Army, 1947), 65. Also available online from http://www.history.hqusareur.army.mil/Archives/First Year/the first year 1.pdf; accessed 10 February 2006.

19. Ziemke, 354-5.

20. Frederiksen,121.

21. Pre-occupation Germany was organized into a patchwork of large noncontiguous states (Prussia and Bavaria) and smaller political entities left over from the 19th century unification of Germany. Before being reorganized into the present Federal Republic states (*Länder*) of Bavaria, Hesse, and

Baden-Württemberg, the territory that became the American sector consisted of Bavaria, the northern half of the states of Baden and Württemberg, which were organized into a new state, Württemberg-Baden, and Hesse, a new state formed by consolidation of the portion of the former state of Hesse-Darmstadt not in the French sector, the city of Frankfurt-am-Main and the former Prussian province of Electoral Hesse, (*Kurhessen*) and portions of the former Prussian province of Nassau not in the French sector. These new states were officially organized in September 1945 with German state governments. (See "First Year," vol. 1, 99.) In 1952 Württemberg-Baden was merged with two states from the former French sector, Baden and Württemberg–Hohenzollern, to form the new state of Baden-Württemberg. For a good map of the provinces and their relationship to the American sector, see Map 3 inside the back cover of Ziemke.

22. Ziemke,118, 396, 417. The 1939 German census counted a population of 17,864,000 in the US zone. See Donald R. Whitnah and Edgar L. Erickson, *The American Occupation of Austria: Planning and Early Years*, (Westport, CT: Greenwood Press, 1985), 91-2.

23. Frederiksen, 12; Historical Division, European Command, "The Third Year of the Occupation, First Quarter: 1 July-30 September 1947", in *Occupation Forces in Europe Series, 1947-48* (Frankfurt, Germany: US Army, 1947), 2. The 19 million population figure includes 500,000 DPs, although up to 2.5 million DPs were in the American zone in the early days of the occupation.

24. Ziemke, 320. Frederiksen, 50. Ziemke gives the total theater strength as 3,077,000. Frederiksen's figure of 3,069,310 is used in this work because he supports the figure with accompanying tables and other statistics. A listing of the divisions in Germany on V-E Day is found in table B-1, appendix B. References for this table are: *European Theater, US Army, Order of Battle of the United States Army, World War II, European Theater of Operations: Divisions* (Office of the Theater Historian, Paris,1945); John Wilson, comp. *Armies, Corps, Divisions, and Separate Brigades*, Army Lineage Series, CMH Pub 60-7(Washington, DC: US Army Center of Military History, 1999).

25. The disbanded army headquarters was the 9th. The army headquarters redeployed was the 1st, the three corps headquarters were the III, VII, and XIII, and the 11 divisions were the 2d, 4th, 5th, 8th, 44th, 86th, 95th, 97th, and 104th Infantry Divisions and the 13th and 20th Armored Divisions. See Shelby Stanton, *Order of Battle, U.S. Army, World War II* (Novato, CA: Presidio, 1984).

26. "First Year," vol. 1, 52-3, 122; Ziemke, 334.

27. Ziemke, 320-1, 334-5, 339. The designated occupation divisions were the 1st, 3d, 9th, 42d, and 78th Infantry Divisions and the 1st and 4th Armored Divisions, with the eighth division equivalent made up of several separate regiments and battalions. See "First Year," vol. 1, 133. The original OTB numbers included Army Air Force elements. Actual ground troop numbers were 285,000, of which only 144,000 were tactical troops, the remainder were headquarters, service, or administrative troops. See "First Year," vol. 1, 142.

28. Ibid.; Frederiksen, 84. Over five million tons of excess and captured materiel had already been liquidated following the German surrender.

29. "First Year," vol. 1, 121-2, 128, 133.

30. See footnote 22; Ziemke, 341. A force of 38,000 US troops at a ratio of 1:450 Germans gives a rough population estimate of 17.1 million. The prewar (1939) census was 17.86 million. Actual population estimates for the American zone, including DPs and prisoners of war (POW) in 1945 were 19 million. Planners presumably estimated the DP, POW, non-German, and wartime population would decline resulting in a decrease in population of 1.9 million. Approximately 38,000 constables in a population of 17.1 million locals produces a ratio of 2.2 troopers per inhabitant. One source claims theater planners used an area basis for force size determination, estimating one 140-man unit for every 225 square miles of occupied territory. But the math for this estimate is not apparent. With a zone area of 45,600 square miles, this estimate would require 203, 140-man units. Presuming these units equate to a Constabulary troop, with five troops per squadron, this indicates a requirement for 41 squadrons; only 27 were deployed. Including the companies and artillery batteries in the three tactical divisions to be retained, this only adds about 36 more units to the 135 of the Constabulary, still 40 below the 203 figure. See Robert Cameron, "There and Back Again: Constabulary Training and Organization, 1946-1950" in *Armed Diplomacy: Two Centuries of American Campaigning* (paper presented at conference sponsored by US Army Training and Doctrine Command, Fort Leavenworth, KS, 5-7 August 2003), (Fort Leavenworth: Combat Studies Institute Press, 2003), 120-1. These planning figures are discussed again in the conclusion to this work.

31. "First Year," vol. 1, 136, 143.

32. Historical Division, European Command, US Army, "The Third Year of the Occupation, First Quarter," in *Occupation Forces in Europe Series*, vol. 1 (Frankfurt, Germany: US Army, 1947), 9. The logisticians and personnel specialists were the ones who estimated the duration of the occupation. Supply stocks were maintained with a projected end date of 1 August 1947. After the projected 1 July 1950 termination date of the Constabulary, it was projected that an infantry division would be retained until the end of the occupation.

33. Office of the Chief Historian, European Command, "The Second Year of the Occupation" in *Occupation Forces in Europe Series, 1946-1947*, vol. 1 (Frankfurt, Germany: US Army, 1947), 136.

34. "Second Year," vol. 1, 23-4. By spring 1946, there were only four divisions remaining in Germany, the 1st, 3rd, and 9th Infantry Divisions and the 4th Armored Division. On 1 July 1946 the 4th Armored Division and the remaining cavalry groups were reorganized as the US Constabulary. The 3d Infantry Division rotated to the US in September 1946 and the 9th Infantry Division was inactivated in January 1947. This left only the Constabulary, the 1st Infantry Division, and several separate infantry battalions and companies in Europe.

35. "Second Year," vol. 1, 63.

36. Office of the Chief Historian, European Command, "The Second Year of the Occupation" in *Occupation Forces in Europe Series, 1946-1947*, vol. V (Frankfurt, Germany: US Army, 1947), 18.

37. "Third Year, First Quarter," vol. 1, 6.

38. Ibid., 3-4.

39. Kendall Gott, *Mobility, Vigilance, and Justice: The US Army Constabulary in Germany, 1946-1953*, Global War on Terrorism Occasional Paper 11 (Fort Leavenworth: Combat Studies Press, 2005), 26-28; Cameron, 120, 131-3. Although the Constabulary had used the cavalry terms squadron and troop for unit designations, the new armored cavalry regiments used 'battalion' and 'company' until 1960.

40. As of 31 December 1951, the US Seventh Army consisted of the V Corps (1st and 4th Infantry Divisions and the 2d Armored Division) and the VII Corps (28th and 43d Infantry Divisions). A new command, United States European Command (USEUCOM) was established to control all US forces. The former EUCOM, an Army organization, was redesignated US Army Europe (USAREUR). Additionally, US forces in Germany were placed under a new Central Army Group which included both the Seventh Army and French forces. This group corresponded to the Northern Army Group, which included the British, Dutch, and Belgian units in northern West Germany.

41. The military post organizational system was adopted along with the police-type occupation plan. During the army-type occupation period, a system of military communities had been used, where the local tactical units were in charge of the communities.

42. During the early occupation there was an Eastern District (Bavaria) and Western District (Hesse and Württemberg-Baden). Seventh Army was in charge of the Western District, and Third Army was in charge of the Eastern District. The districts were later converted to Army Areas and then eliminated completely by early 1946. See "First Year," vol. 1, 53, 149.

43. "Second Year," vol. V, 3, 5, 13.

44. Frederiksen, 195, 32-33, 35.

45. Gott, 15.

46. United States Armed Forces Information School, *The Army Almanac: A Book of Facts Concerning the Army of the United States* (Washington, DC: Government Printing Office, 1950), 763.

47. Historical Division, European Command, US Army, "The Evolution of the Occupation Forces in Europe," in *Occupation Forces in Europe Series*, (Frankfurt, Germany: US Army, 1948), extract found at "The Immediate Post-War Period, May 1945-June 1946," *USFA-History* website, available at http://www.usfava.com/USFA_History1.htm; Internet; accessed 7 October 2005.

48. Second Year," vol. V, 18; "USFA Timeline," *USFA History;* online; available at http://www.usfava.com/USFA_Timeline.htm; Internet; accessed 7 October 2005. The 88th Infantry Division which had been garrisoning Trieste in Italy until 1947 and one of its regiments, the 351st Infantry, remained there until 1954.

49. William Stacey, *US Army Border Operations in Germany 1945-1983* (Heidelberg, Germany: US Army Europe and Seventh Army, 1984), 13-4, 33.

50. "Third Year, First Quarter," vol. 1, 3, 9.

51. William Stearman, *The Soviet Union and the Occupation of Austria: An Analysis of Soviet Policy in Austria, 1945-1955* (Bonn, Germany: Siegler, 1961), 59.

52. A tabulation of the initial troops deployed for the occupation of Japan is found in table B-2, appendix B. In addition to these troops, the XXIV Corps was in Korea with the 6th, 7th, and 40th Infantry Divisions.

53. For example, initially near Tokyo were the Americal Division, 1st Cavalry Division, 43d Infantry Division, and the 112th Cavalry Regiment.

54. For more information on the British Commonwealth forces see "Brief History of Australia's Participation in the Occupation of Japan, 1945–1952," *British Commonwealth Occupation Forces National Council* [document on-line] available at http://www.bradprint.com.au/bcof/history.html; Internet; accessed 11 October 2005. A tabulation of US troop reductions in Japan is found in table B-3, appendix B.

55. James Dobbins, John G. McGinn, Keith Crane, Seth G. Jones, Rollie Lal, Andrew Rathmell, Rachel Swanger, and Anga Timilsina, *America's Role in Nation-Building: From Germany to Iraq.* MR-1753 (Santa Monica, CA: Rand, 2003), 27-8, 38-42 [report on-line] available at http://www.rand.org/publications/MR/MR1753/; Internet; accessed 27 January 2005.

56. *The Army Almanac*, 770-71; "Brief History of Australia's Participation in the Occupation of Japan 1945-1952."

57. "Brief History of Australia's Participation in the Occupation of Japan 1945-1952." The remaining US force structure included the Eighth Army headquarters and two corps headquarters (I and IX), which were inactivated in early 1950, and reactivated for the Korean War, the 1st Cavalry, and 24th and 25th Infantry Divisions. In 1948 the 7th Infantry Division was shifted from South Korea to Japan to replace the 11th Airborne Division which redeployed back to the United States. During this period, the 24th Infantry Division replaced its 4th Infantry Regiment with the all-black 24th Infantry Regiment. The 1st Cavalry Division eliminated the command echelon of brigade and one of its four infantry regiments, the 12th Cavalry. By 1949 all the infantry divisions, (except the 25th where the segregated 24th Infantry had all three battalions and a full strength direct support artillery battalion) were short a battalion each in their three organic infantry regiments, and lacked organic reconnaissance elements and a firing battery from each organic direct support field artillery battalion. See John Wilson, *Maneuver and Firepower: The Evolution of Divisions and Separate Brigades* (Washington, DC: US Army Center of Military History, 1998), 239.

58. The population figure is as of 1 October 1945 as calculated by the Statistics Bureau, Management and Coordination Agency, Government of Japan. Area is interpolated from the same data via population density figures. See *Selected Demographic Indicators for Japan*, http://www.ipss.go.jp/p=info/e/S_D_1/Indip.html; Internet; accessed 10 October 2005.

59. The geographical description of Japan comes primarily from *A Country Study: Japan*, Library of Congress Country Studies, [document online] available at http://lcweb2.loc.gov/frd/cs/jptoc.html; Internet; accessed 12 October 2005.

60. Theodore Cohen, *Remaking Japan: The American Occupation as New Deal*, Herbert Passin, ed. (New York: Free Press, 1988), 60.

61. Howard Schonberger, *Aftermath of War: Americans and the Remaking of Japan, 1945-1952* (Kent, OH: Kent State University Press, 1989), 48.

62. Dobbins et al., 34; "Brief History of Australia's Participation in the Occupation of Japan 1945-1952;" *The Army Almanac,* 633. For a breakdown by division of the downsizing, see note 52. For a discussion of the size of the US divisions see note 55.

63. Dobbins et al., 42-3.

64. Robert Jackson, *The Malayan Emergency: The Commonwealth's Wars 1948-1966* (New York: Routledge, 1991), 10-11.

65. John Scurr, *The Malayan Campaign, 1948-60.* Illustrated by Mike Chappell. Men-at-Arms series (London: Osprey, 1982), 4; Jackson, 12-13, 25, 59.

66. John Coates, *Suppressing Insurgency: An Analysis of the Malayan Emergency, 1948-1954* (Boulder, CO: Westview Press, 1992), 37, 149-50, 159.

67. Ibid., 35.

68. Jackson, 28-9.

69. Ibid., 30-31, 37.

70. Coates, 80.

71. Jackson, 20; Scurr,14.

72. Scurr,19; Coates, 156.

73. Coates, 84, 129; Jackson, 22-3.

74. Scurr, 14; Coates 96.

75. Coates, 186; Jackson, 24.

76. Coates, 118-9, 186; "The History of the British Army: Malaya 1950-1957," *National Army Museum* website, http://www.national-army-museum.ac.uk/pages/malaya.html; Internet; accessed 9 September 2005. Templer is reputed to have coined the much-repeated phrase "winning the hearts and minds."

77. Jackson, 23, 47, 57; Coates, 94.

78. Coates, 185-6. As early as December 1952, Templer himself recognized the end was in sight. On the cover of the 5 December 1952 issue of *Time* magazine he was quoted as declaring, "The jungle has been neutralized."

79. Templer is reputed as saying: "I'll shoot the bastard who says that this Emergency is over."

80. Scurr, 30-1; Jackson, 53, 57, 59-60.

81. Coates, 143-4; Jackson, 1-2; Charles Hirschman, "The Society and Its Environment" in *Malaysia: A Country Study,* Frederick M. Bunge, ed. (Washington, DC: Department of the Army, 1984) 70-1, 74.

82. Scurr, 3.

83. Ibid.

84. Jackson, 18-19; Coates, 168. British and Commonwealth brigade and battalion deployment for the Malayan Emergency is indicated in table B-4, appendix B. Unit abbreviations used in figure 9 are defined in that table.

85. "National Service and the Post-1949 British Army," *The History of the*

British Army; available at http://www.national-army-museum.ac.uk/pages/nat-service.html; Internet; accessed 6 September 2005.

86. Jackson, 45-7; Coates, 33.

87. Scurr, 25.

88. "Brigade of Gurkhas History," *The Brigade of Gurkhas* [document-on-line] available at http://www.army.mod.uk/linked_files/gurkhas/The_World_Wars_and_the_subsequent_hisory.doc; Internet; accessed 6 September 2005. (Editor's note: The word 'history' has been incorrectly spelled in the web address for this citation. The web address is correct as listed here.)

89. "The Brigade of Gurkhas-Background Information," *The Brigade of Gurkhas* [document-on-line] available at http://www.army.mod.uk/brigade_of_gurkhas/history/brigade_background.htm; Internet: accessed 6 September 2005.

90. Coates,166-7. The Fijian and East African units, made up of volunteers and regular officers were the only Commonwealth units with a performance superior to the Gurkhas. The British battalions, with their conscripts and rotational schemes, while still performing at a high level of efficiency, were relatively speaking, the least effective of the various types of Commonwealth forces operating in Malaya.

91. Ibid., 166.

92. Ibid., 122; Jackson, 49. The one battalion in the Federation Regiment as of May 1954 was composed of 50 percent British officers, 25 percent Chinese officers, while the remaining 25 percent were Indian, Malay, or Eurasian officers. The enlisted ranks were 43 percent Malay, 33 percent Chinese, 19 percent Indian, and 5 percent other. See Coates, 139.

93. Coates, 100.

94. Scurr, 8.

95. Jackson, 44, 54.

96. Ibid., 85, 116.

97. Scurr, 6; Jackson, 17-8; Coates, 92, 123, 165.

98. Jackson, 25; Coates, 49, 124-5, 157, 183-4.

99. Coates, 120-1, 124; "The History of the British Army: Malaya 1950-1957"; Jackson, 20.

100. In 2003 Serbia and Montenegro formed a new, looser union to replace the new Yugoslavia. The new state is called simply Serbia and Montenegro.

101. Army in Europe (AE) Pamphlet 525-100, *The U.S. Army in Bosnia and Herzegovina* (Heidelberg, Germany: US Army Europe, Seventh Army, 2003) 22-4 [document on-line] available at http://www.fas.org/irp/doddir/army/ae-pam-525-100.pdf; Internet; accessed 17 October 2005; Dobbins et al., 98.

102. Jim Garamore, "Ending War, Enforcing Peace in Bosnia," *Defenselink News*, 2 December 2004, [article on-line] available at http://www.defenselinknews.mil/news/Dec2004/n12022004_2004120208.html; Internet; accessed 17 October 2005; Dobbins et al., 97-98.

103. Central Intelligence Agency, "Bosnia and Herzegovina," World

Factbook, [document on-line] available at http://www.cia.gov/cia/publications/factbook/geos/bk.html; Internet; accessed 13 October 2005.

104. For example, while MND-N was always commanded by a US division staff, as part of the IFOR it initially included two American brigades, an American aviation brigade, a Russian brigade, a Turkish brigade as well as a brigade of troops from the Scandinavian countries and Poland and support troops from Hungary and Romania. Due to downsizing, these contingents, as part of the SFOR, were reduced in size over time but contained contingents from the same nations throughout. See *US Army in Bosnia, 23*. The British division (MND-SW) typically contained a British brigade, a Canadian brigade, and battalions from the Czech Republic, the Netherlands, and Malaysia. The French division typically included a French brigade, a Spanish brigade, and an Italian brigade, with battalions from Portugal, Egypt, and the Ukraine. For a snapshot IFOR order of battle from September 1996 see "IFOR: Participating Forces," *The Balkan Conflict*, http://home.wandoo.nl/tcc/balkan/ifor_forces.html; Internet; accessed 17 October 2005.

105. *US Army in Bosnia* 23, 27, 33. The reaction force was known as the Multinational Specialized Unit (MSU) and was used primarily to clear mines or other special missions related to public security beyond the present capability of local forces. Base camp density in the US (MND-N) sector is found in table B-5, appendix B.

106. Ibid.,16.

107. Ibid., 27.

108. Dobbins et al., 97.

109. "Bosnia's Stalled Police Reform: No Progress, No EU," *International Crisis Group Europe Report,* no. 164, 6 September 2005 [report on-line] available at http://www.crisisgroup.org/home/index.cfm?id=3645&l=1; Internet; accessed 18 October 2005.

110. At the height of the Bosnian conflict, out of a total population of four million, as many as 430,000 troops were armed. Both forces, based on the example of the former Yugoslav army, did not have a divisional echelon of command. Accordingly, brigades reported directly to corps headquarters. "Army of Bosnia and Herzegovina: Order of Battle 1995," October 2004 [website on-line] available at http://www.vojska.net/military/bih/armija/orbat/1995/default.asp; Internet; accessed 18 October 2005; "Army of Republic of Srpska: Order of Battle, 1992-1995," September 2003 [website on-line] available at http://www.vojska.net/military/bih/vrs/oob/1995.asp; Internet; accessed 18 October 2005; "Bosnia's Next Five Years: Dayton and Beyond" November 2000 [document on-line] available at http://www.usip.org/pubs/specialreports/sr001103.html; Internet; accessed 17 October 2005; "The Armed Forces in Bosnia and Herzegovina," *EUFOR: European Union Force in Bosnia and Herzegovina* [website on-line] available at http://www.euforbih.org/bih/tchapter4.htm; Internet; accessed 18 October 2005.

111. "Background to the Conflict," *Official Site of the Kosovo Force* [website on-line] available at http://www.nato.int/kfor/kfor/intro.htm; Internet; accessed 19 October 2005.

112. "Briefing by the Defence Secretary and Mr. George Robertson and the Deputy Chief of the Defence Staff (Commitments), Air Marshal Sir John Day," (press briefing at the London Ministry of Defence, 26 May 1999) [press briefing on-line] available at http://www.kosovo.mod.uk/brief260599.htm; Internet; accessed 19 October 2005. It has been estimated that over one million ethnic Albanians, or about half the population, had fled their homes by June 1999. See Dobbins et al., 113.

113. "KFOR Press Update," (press briefing by Major Roland Lavoie, KFOR Spokesperson in Pristina, Kosovo, 30 August 1999) [press briefing on-line] available at http://www.nato.int/kosovo/press/1999/k990830a.htm; Internet; accessed 19 October 2005. For other strength figures see Dobbins et al., 115 and "Operation Joint Guardian, Kosovo Force (KFOR)," March 2005 [website on-line] available at http://www.globalsecurity.org/military/ops/joint_guardian.htm; Internet; accessed 19 October 2005.

114. "Robertson Briefing," 26 May 1999."

115. For the original planned rotations, see "Army Announces Updated Balkans Rotation Schedule," 4 December 2000 [press release on-line] available at http://www4.army.mil/ocpa/read.php?story_id_key=1761; Internet; accessed 20 October 2005. US forces deployed in support of KFOR and MND-E from 1999 to 2005 are listed in table B-6, appendix B. The force package was known as Task Force Falcon.

116. Dobbins et al.,126.

117. "KFOR Headquarters," September 2005 [document on-line] available at http://www.nato.int/kfor/kfor/kfor_hq.htm; Internet; accessed 19 October 2005; "Press conference by NATO Secretary General Jaap de Hoop Scheffer," (press conference by NATO Secretary General Jaap de Hoop Scheffer in Pristina, Kosovo, 13 May 2005) May 2005 [press briefing on-line] available at http://www. nato.int/docu/speech/2005/s050513a.htm; Internet; accessed 19 October 2005.

118. "Kosovo and its Population," [document on-line] available at http:// www.sok-kosovo.org/pdf/population/Kosovo_population.pdf; Internet; accessed 13 February 2006.

119. Dobbins et al., 113.

120. KFOR command by nationality is listed in table B-7, appendix B. This information was culled from "Kosovo Force (KFOR), Official Website of the Kosovo Force," [website on-line] available at http://www.nato.int/kfor/welcome. html; Internet; accessed 19 October 2005.

121. "KFOR Headquarters."

122. Also see Note 116. "Press Club, October 10, 2002," *Task Force Falcon website*, [website on-line] available at http://www.tffalcon.hqusareur.army. mil/Media/PRESS_CLUB/PC10oct02.pdf; Internet; accessed 19 October 2005. There were some initial problems with US force commanders not wanting to cross sector boundaries, but these issues were soon resolved. See Dobbins et al., 118.

123. Dobbins et al., 113, 116.

124. Ibid., 118-9; "Kosovo Protection Corps," [website on-line] available at

http://www.unmikonline.org/1styear/kpcorps.htm; Internet; accessed 19 October 2005. UNMIK is the UN Mission in Kosovo, established in June 1999 to administer Kosovo until a stable civilian administration could be established.

125. See endnote 122.

126. Dobbins et al., 119-120.

Chapter 3
Police Departments
Introduction

This work will now discuss civilian police departments in the United States and determine how they are organized in relation to the population density and geographical area in which each department maintains law and order. Additionally, the rationale behind the size of the departments and their effectiveness will be analyzed. For the purposes of this study, the police precinct (or equivalent) is considered the equivalent of the military battalion and the police division (or equivalent) will be considered the equivalent of a military brigade.

New York City

The New York Police Department (NYPD) was established in 1898 in its present form, when the merger of the city of New York (Manhattan and the Bronx), the city of Brooklyn, the various towns, and localities of the county of Queens and the county of Richmond (Staten Island) formed the greater city of New York.

Geographical Area and Terrain

New York City sprawls across 308.9 square miles and is located on two islands (Manhattan and Staten Island), part of a third (Long Island), and a large area, the Bronx, on the New York state mainland.

Population Density

According to the 2000 national census, the population of New York City is just over eight million (8,008,278), making it the largest city in the United States. The population density for the whole city is 25,925 inhabitants per square mile. While this citywide average is by far the densest of any major US city, certain parts of New York City are more densely settled than others. For example, the borough of Manhattan has a population of 1,537,195 (19.2 percent of the city's total population). However, the land area of Manhattan is only 23 square miles or slightly less than 8 percent of the total land area of the city. This gives Manhattan a population density of 66,834 persons per square mile, more than twice the population density of the city as a whole. In contrast, the borough of Staten Island has a population of 378,977 (5.2 percent of the city's population) in 58 square miles, more than twice the size of Manhattan and has a population density of 6534 residents per square mile.[1]

Ratio of Police Officers to Population

The New York Police Department is the largest municipal police department in the United States and, as of 2003, had 39,110 members.[2] This large size enables the New York Police Department theoretically to deploy 126.7 police officers per square mile of city and to provide 1 officer for every 205 city residents. This also reflects the unique characteristics of New York City where the overall population density is double the population density of the second and third most densely populated cities, Chicago and Boston. A large population in a relatively small area results in a high level of congestion, making rapid movement around the city by motor vehicle impossible at certain times. The low ratio of motor vehicles to police officers is reflective of this congestion and the long tradition of officers "walking a beat." The New York Police Department operates roughly 4656 patrol cars.[3] This provides approximately 1 car for every 8.4 police officers. Assuming officers on the traditional three eight-hour shifts (0800-1600, 1600-2400, 2400-0800) share the vehicles, the ratio decreases to 2.7 officers per vehicle, leaving about every third police officer on foot even under optimum conditions.

NYPD Organizational Structure

The basic unit of the New York Police Department is the precinct, consisting of between 200 and 500 officers and commanded (in rising order of seniority) by a police captain, deputy inspector, or inspector. Under the current organization, the New York Police Department operates 76 precincts and 12 additional transit districts roughly equivalent to precincts. Thus, across the force, an NYPD precinct has an average 444 officers. Precincts are geographical commands responsible for a specific territory. This area varies primarily based on population density. The smallest precinct area has less than one-half square mile (containing 35,500 residents), and the largest has 8.12 square miles in area. Grouped within eight patrol boroughs, the precincts are roughly equivalent in size to Army brigades. Patrol boroughs control between 8 and 13 precincts, except for the Staten Island Patrol Borough, which controls only the three precincts on the relatively less densely populated island. Assistant chiefs (the grade higher than inspector and the highest grade to command a precinct) command patrol boroughs.[4] Figure 14 shows the geographical layout of the NYPD's organizational structure.

NYPD Operational Successes

In the 1990s the New York Police Department enjoyed great operational success as the New York crime rate and murder rates dropped

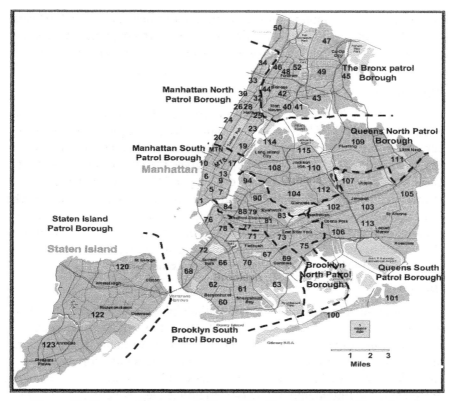

Figure 14. Geographical organization of the New York Police Department.

dramatically. During these years, the department adopted a decentralized operational plan where each precinct commander fought crime in his own precinct using trends, statistics, and other data compiled by a computerized tracking system called COMPSTAT.

Other Major Police Departments[5]

Chicago

Long referred to as "the Second City," the city of Chicago, as of 2000, is the third largest city by population in the United States with 2,896,016 residents. However, in population density it ranks second, with an average of 12,746 residents packed into the city's 227.2 square mile area. Accordingly, the Chicago Police Department, with 13,423 officers, ranks second only to the New York Police Department in size, fielding about 59 police officers per square mile of city and providing 1 officer per 218 city residents, or 4.6 officers per 1000 population. Organizationally, each of Chicago's 25 police districts is divided into three subordinate patrol sectors.[6]

71

Each patrol sector contains between three and five beats, totaling 280 beats citywide. Each beat has eight or nine patrol officers assigned to patrol the area on foot, by bicycle, or by vehicle. Overseeing the 25 districts are six area headquarters, including a special command in downtown Chicago.[7]

Philadelphia

The city of Philadelphia, with an area of 135.1 square miles and a population of 1,517,510, has a population density slightly less than the population density of Chicago. The Philadelphia Police Department has a deployed strength of 6728 officers. This gives the city a ratio of 49.8 officers per square mile and 1 police officer per 217.9 city residents, or 4.4 officers per 1000 people. The city is divided into 24 police districts, a park district, and an airport district. Six geographical divisions oversee the operations of the districts.[8] Police patrolling in Philadelphia have traditionally emphasized foot and bicycle patrol, with specialized bike units of 10 officers patrolling particular areas around the clock.[9]

Boston

Boston, as densely populated as Philadelphia and Chicago, is unlike most major US cities because it did not annex most of its inner suburbs. Therefore, the Boston city proper has a rather small area of 48.4 square miles and a population of 589,141.[10] Despite the small population, the city's density of 12,172 residents per square mile is similar to the density of Chicago and Philadelphia. The Boston Police Department is, accordingly, smaller, with 2044 officers. This deployed strength gives Boston a ratio of 42.2 officers per square mile and 1 police officer per 296.7 residents or 3.5 officers per 1000 population.

Los Angeles

The Anomaly of Los Angeles

Los Angeles is the exact opposite of the previously cited cities. Los Angeles has a large geographical area, but a low population density. The city's 3.6 million population sprawls out over 466.8 square miles, giving a density of 7915 residents per square mile, half the density of Chicago, Boston and Philadelphia and almost one-quarter the density of New York City.[11] The 9195-member Los Angeles Police Department provides a ratio of 19.7 police officers per square mile, and a deployed force of 1 officer per 431.2 residents, a proportion of 2.49 police officers per 1000 city residents.[12] Both geographically and demographically, these figures are far smaller than any other major municipal police force in the United States. While the population of Los Angeles is slightly less than half the population of New York City and the area is one and a half times larger, the Los Angeles Police Department is less than a quarter the size of the New York Police Department. Chicago has three-fourths the population of Los Angeles and slightly less than half the land area and has a police force 70 percent larger. Philadelphia has an area one-fourth smaller, less than half the population, and deploys a police force almost three-fourths the size of the Los Angeles Police Department (LAPD). Why do public officials in Los Angeles feel they can deploy a police force substantially smaller proportionally than the police forces of other large American cities? In fact, police officials in Los Angeles have noted the proportionally smaller size of their police department, but a variety of factors has contributed to the LAPD's size.

LAPD Organizational Structure

The first key factor is the LAPD's organizational structure. Based on the population distribution and area of the city, the LAPD's 19 organizational subunits called area divisions are roughly equivalent to the NYPD precincts.[13] Division geographical size varies from 4 square miles to 65 square miles, based primarily on demographics. Large sections within the LA city limits are either undeveloped parkland or upper or middle class suburban neighborhoods. The geographic area of these divisions is larger than the divisions found in the more densely populated inner city sections of Los Angeles.

Typical area division strength is about 350 officers, which includes three major subcomponents, simply called divisions: detective, traffic, and patrol. The patrol divisions are divided into patrol districts. Each patrol division has from 5 to 13 patrol districts. For each work shift, or watch, each patrol district is assigned one patrol car. Overall, as of 2005, the Los Angeles Police Department operated 170 patrol districts throughout the city. At a minimum, each district operates a dedicated patrol car, usually manned by two officers. This patrol, operating on three shifts, or watches, is on duty 24 hours a day. A senior police officer, usually in the grade of sergeant, commands several patrol districts together. Above this sergeant is a lieutenant who leads the entire patrol watch for the specific division.

The size of patrol districts depends on the population density, the geography of the terrain, and the crime rate in the area. Citywide, the proportion of patrol units to population is one patrol unit for every 21,734 residents. District by district, the ratio can vary plus or minus several thousand residents from the citywide figure. Since patrol units are usually two-officer teams, this gives a proportion of one officer to 10,867 residents at the point of the police spear, or one-tenth of a patrol officer per 1000 population. While patrol areas vary in size, the average size of a patrol area citywide is 2.7 square miles. In places where the population is

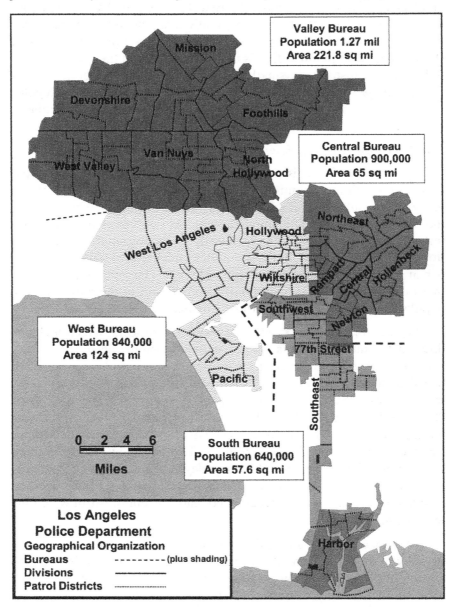

Figure 15. Geographical organization of the Los Angeles Police Department.

more dense, such as the Rampart Division, the patrol districts are smaller, an average of 1.6 square miles.[14] Figure 15 illustrates the geographic organization of the Los Angeles Police Department by bureau, division, and patrol district.

Mobility and the Los Angeles Police Department

Another key factor affecting the size of the Los Angeles Police Department is its high rate of motorization. Los Angeles is both large in population and in geographical area. As previously referenced, the city's population density is far below the densities of New York, Chicago, Philadelphia, and Boston.[15] However, even in areas of Los Angeles where the population density is equal to that of other cities, the ratio of officers to every 1000 residents remains relatively low. For example in the Rampart division (43,750 residents per square mile) and the Newton division (16,666 residents per square mile), the ratio of officers to 1000 residents is 1.0 and 2.3 respectively. This compares to other cities with rates ranging between 3.4 and 4.9 officers per 1000 residents.

A major reason for the smaller ratio is the LAPD's dependence on motorized vehicles. As of 2002, the LAPD's fleet consisted of 4180 patrol cars, 1376 unmarked vehicles, 359 motorcycles, and 17 helicopters.[16] This number of vehicles gives the Los Angeles Police Department an average of one vehicle for every 1.6 police officers. In contrast, the New York Police Department has one vehicle for every eight officers. Counting the marked and unmarked patrol cars together, the Los Angeles Police Department has a pool of more patrol vehicles than the New York Police Department, a force whose personnel strength is 77 percent larger. Despite this large number of vehicles, the sheer geographical size of the city of Los Angeles has resulted in the Los Angeles Police Department deploying an average of about 12 police vehicles for every square mile of city area, less than the averages in each of the five major cities in this study. For example, New York, even while providing only one vehicle for every eight officers, still deployed 15 vehicles per square mile.

A population sprawled over a large area gave the Los Angeles Police Department a traditional appreciation for conducting patrol operations primarily from vehicles. Even though Los Angeles had an early tradition of police walking beats in the downtown areas of the city, the demise of the city's extensive trolley car system after World War II left Los Angeles without an equivalent of the rapid transit subway and elevated railway systems found in the other cities.[17] The motor vehicle became the Los Angeles equivalent. Even while police departments nationwide adopt a generalized doctrine of law enforcement strategy called "community policing," which emphasizes foot and bicycle patrols, the Los Angeles version of community policing still depends on the patrol vehicle as the primary mode of transportation for police officers making local contact with the public.[18]

Table 7 shows a comparison of the motor vehicle deployments of the five municipal police departments studied in this section. From this table it can be deduced the Los Angeles Police Department has a proportion of vehicles per officer almost three times the average. This disparity in the number of officers per vehicle may provide a rationale for the proportional size difference between the Los Angeles Police Department (2.5 officers per 1000 people) and the average size of the other four police departments (4.35 officers per 1000 people), which, on average deploy almost twice as many officers (a difference of 1.85 officers per 1000 residents).

Table 7. US Municipal Police Force Vehicle Density

	Size of Force	Number of Patrol Vehicles	Ratio of Officers to Vehicles	Ratio of Vehicles per 1000 Residents	Ratio of Vehicles to Area (square miles)
New York	39,100	4656[19]	8.3	0.58	15.07
Chicago	13,289	2982[20]	4.5	1.02	17.61
Philadelphia	6728	1500[21]	4.5	1.01	11.10
Boston	2044	698[22]	2.9	1.18	14.42
Los Angeles	9195	5556[23]	1.6	1.50	11.90
Averages			4.4	1.06	14.02

Crime Rates in Los Angeles

Subsequent to the 1950s, despite rising crime rates in Los Angeles and across the nation, the size of the Los Angeles Police Department only increased as the population increased. It was only during the 1970s the police department reached its current staff level of 2.5 officers per 1000 city residents.[24]

Though the crime rate in Los Angeles did increase, it remained low relative to other cities. The relatively low crime rate in Los Angeles seemed to indicate the size of the Los Angeles Police Department was adequate. Although the police force was proportionally smaller than most other major cities, the LA crime rate was lower than the crime rates in cities with larger police forces. In 2002, for example, of the five cities studied here, only New York had a lower crime rate. In fact, of all large American cities (over one million in population), in 2002 only New York and San Diego had lower crime rates.[25]

Coupled with low crime rates, a belief existed, prevalent among municipal officials and senior police officers, that the high level of professionalism in the Los Angeles Police Department made it possible to do more with fewer officers, something not possible in other cities. LA public officials and police commanders prided themselves on using their resources proactively and creatively. For example, former LAPD chief Daryl Gates boasted in his memoirs the department, per officer, averaged 3.1 arrests for violent crime per year in contrast to a rate of 1.8 for the New York Police Department.[26]

Additionally, while their police department was proportionally smaller than similar departments elsewhere, the people of Los Angeles still believed their government was excessively large and needed to downsized. This was most apparent in proposed secession movements in Hollywood and the San Fernando Valley in 2002, and as far back as 1978 when the passage of State Proposition 13 actually cut LAPD personnel strength for a period of time.[27] Even Gates, while acknowledging the small size of the force, stated the public should not be expected to allocate any more funds for police than those already budgeted.[28]

LA Police Officials and Police Density

Traditionally, Los Angeles has never deployed a police force much larger than its present 2.5 police officers per 1000 residents. While many LAPD officials pride themselves on the ability of the department to do its job with a smaller force, many believe the low proportion of police to LA residents resulted in the force providing the public minimum service while working at maximum capacity at all times.[29]

In 2004 the Los Angeles Police Department, led by Chief William Bratton, who had been highly successful in Boston and New York, began pushing for public funding for modest personnel increases. As outlined in the *Los Angeles Police Department Plan of Action: Book II*, written to support a November 2004 sales tax increase to fund additional law enforcement measures, LAPD officials proposed a 35 percent increase in the size of the force to 12,500 officers.[30] This increase, if implemented, would have resulted in an increase in the ratio of police officers to residents of 1 officer for every 296 residents (3.3 officers per 1000 residents). While still below the levels of most other cities, the LAPD ratio of officers to residents would be a lot closer to the average (4.4 officers per 1000 residents) of the other cities studied in this work. The higher rate of motorization of the Los Angeles Police Department could then compensate for the difference in size without a loss of effectiveness. However, the referendum authorizing the sales tax increase to pay for the personnel increases was defeated at the polls in November 2004. City officials immediately began to look for new ways to fund or otherwise increase the size of the force.[31]

US Major Municipal Police Force Troop Density Summary

Table 8 outlines a comparison between the officer densities of the police departments discussed in this section in terms of demographic, geographic and organizational density. Including the figures projected by LA officials, the average police density is 1 police officer per 248.12 residents or 4.1 officers per 1000 population. Average geographic density is 60.9 officers per square mile.

Organizationally, each police department is divided into smaller subunits, roughly equivalent to an Army company, referred to by various names (precinct, division, or district). The number of subunits seems to be based primarily on demographics, rather than geography, as they vary in geographical size but overall, average 333.2 officers. On the average, these departments organized one of these subunits for every 50,137.5 residents.

What general conclusions can be drawn from this sampling of troop density for municipal police departments? Municipal police departments appear to base their strengths primarily on the size of the population they are supporting rather than on the geographical area they patrol. The more densely populated the city, the higher the police density. The range of densities is between 3.3 and 4.9 police officers per 1000 of population, with an average of 4.1 officers per 1000 residents.[32] To summarize, the higher the population density, the greater the number of police officers per 1000 residents patrolling designated areas. Inversely, the greater the number of motor vehicles operated by the police department (motorization), the fewer police officers per 1000 residents. Figures 16 and 17 depict this inverse relationship.

In terms of geographical area, the range of police densities runs from the LAPD's 19.7 officers per square mile to the NYPD's 126.7 officers per square mile. However, unlike population density, police area densities do not necessarily increase as area increases. Los Angeles has the largest area in the sampling but has the lowest number of officers per square mile.

Table 8. US Municipal Police Force Officer Density[33]

| City | Population | Area | Population Density (per square mile) | Police Force | | Police Density | | |
				Size	Precincts/ Equivalents (average size)	Per Area (officer per square mile)	Per Population (1 per x Residents)	Police per 1000 Residents
Boston	589,141	48.4	12,172	2044	11 (180)	42.2	296.7	3.5
New York	8,008,278	308.9	25,925	39,110	88 (444)	126.7	204.8	4.9
Philadelphia	1,517,550	135.1	11,233	6728	24 (160)	49.8	225.6	4.4
Chicago	2,896,016	227.2	12,746	13,423	25 (532)	59.1	217.9	4.6
Los Angeles								
Current	3,694,820	466.8	7915	9195	19 (350)	19.7	431.2	2.5
Projected				12,500	21 (350)	26.7	295.6	3.3
Average (LA projected figures used)					*(333.2)	60.9	248.12	4.1

*1 subunit for every 50,137.5 residents

79

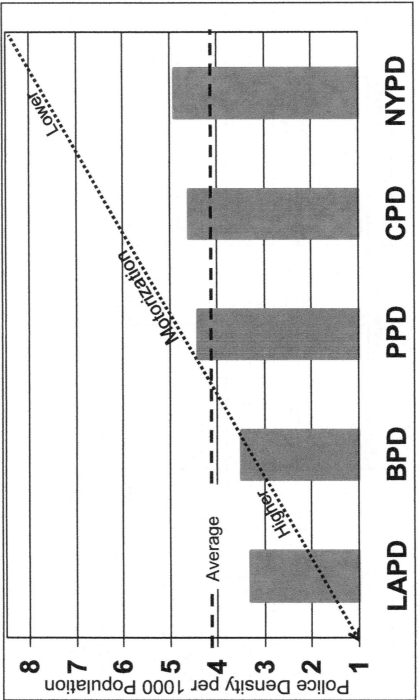

Figure 16. Municipal police department densities by population.

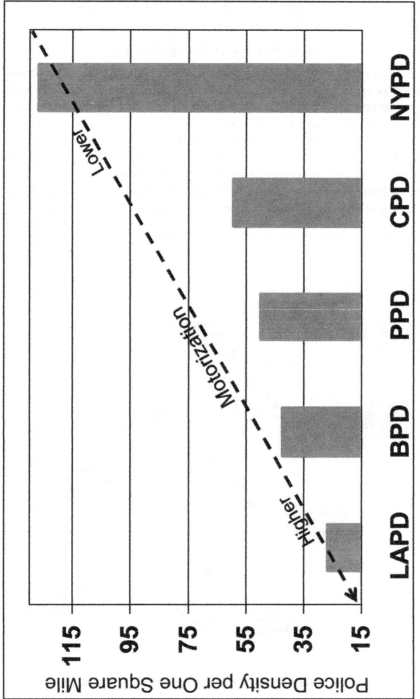

Figure 17. Municipal police department densities by area.

However, as in population density, the greater the rate of motorization of the police department, the fewer officers it deploys per square mile.

State Police Force Troop Density

All US states, with the exception of Hawaii, have state police forces of various sizes. These forces are responsible for conducting statewide law enforcement and traffic control functions beyond those conducted by the local (municipal and county) police. Accordingly, the sizes of state police forces are substantially smaller than police forces in the largest cities. Even the largest state police force, the California Highway Patrol (CHP), with 6678 officers, is exceeded in size by the proportionally small Los Angeles Police Department with 9195 officers.[34] Nevertheless, a brief examination of this largest state police force will provide some insight into

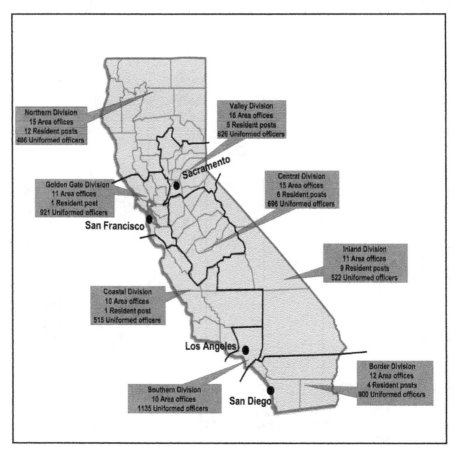

Figure 18. California Highway Patrol geographic organization.

the overall issue of troop density because the California Highway Patrol is responsible for a large geographic area and a total population roughly comparable to Iraq. Additionally, Army planners studied the California Highway Patrol, as well as other municipal California police forces when they determined force requirements for stability operations in Iraq before the start of Operation IRAQI FREEDOM.[35]

The California Highway Patrol augments the law enforcement activities of local municipal and county police forces in the state of California by providing specialized services that transcend local boundaries and by providing traffic control and other activities related to the highways of California. Accordingly, even though it has the nation's largest state police force, the California Highway Patrol is, in proportion, substantially smaller than the average municipal police department. Based on the 2000 census, the population of California is 33,871,648, making it the most populous state. The area of the state is 163,707 square miles, the third largest state after Alaska and Texas. Statewide population density is 206.9 persons per square mile. With trooper strength of 6678, CHP troop density is 0.20 officers per 1000 state residents, or 1 highway patrol officer for every 5,072.12 inhabitants. In terms of area, there is one highway patrol officer for every 24.51 square miles of the state.

As with other police forces, the California Highway Patrol is organized into subordinate units and as illustrated in figure 18, is subdivided into eight geographic divisions.

Between 500 and 1000 officers staff each division. The geographic size of the division and its staffing is dependent on demographics. For example, the largest division in terms of personnel is the Los Angeles area. Statistically, an average division size is 834.75 officers. There is an average of 1 division for every 4.23 million state residents.

Police Density Conclusions

From the sampling of the largest municipal police departments in the United States, police density at the municipal level averages 4.1 officers per 1000 of population, 60.9 officers per municipal square mile and 1 police subunit (precinct equivalent), averaging 333.2 officers, for every 50,137.5 residents. The higher the number of motor vehicles deployed by a police force, the lower its density, both in relation to population and to area of responsibility. Augmenting the municipal forces are state forces. The California Highway Patrol, the largest state police force, adds an average of 0.20 officers per 1000 people, 1 officer per 24.51 square miles, and one additional police subunit (district) with 834.75 officers per 4.23 million residents.

What does this mean for troop density in contingency operations? From this sampling, it is apparent the police density, even for the largest municipal police departments, is far smaller than the densities of the sampling of military forces employed in successful contingency operations. Therefore, it can be concluded routine police operations, even in times of heightened crime, still require a proportionally smaller force than is typical of a contingency operation. However, it can also be concluded that even in a contingency operation, routine police operations will be required and a portion of the troop force roughly equal to the average proportional size of municipal police forces will be necessary to provide minimal police functions during the contingency operation.

Notes

1. New York City Department of City Planning, "Population Division: 2000 Census Summary," [document on-line] available at http://www.ci.nyc.ny.us/html/dcp/html/census/pop2000.shtml; Internet; accessed 25 August 2005.

2. "New York Police Department, "Frequently Asked Questions," [document on-line] available at http://www.nyc.gov/html/nypd/html/misc/pdfaq2.html; Internet; accessed 25 August 2005.

3. Jon LeSage, "Cutting Car Costs," *Police One.com*, 21 April 2005, [document on-line] available at http://www.policeone.com/police-products/vehicle-equipment/articles/99939/; Internet; accessed 25 August 2005.

4. Table B-8, appendix B contains a listing of the NYPD precincts and the relationship between them and demographic and geographic size. The table was compiled from the individual precinct web pages found on the NYPD website (http://www.nyc.gov/html/nypd/). Unlike other police departments, the command grade of an NYPD precinct varies, although no apparent criteria for this variation are discernible. The grades of precinct commanders in order of seniority are inspector, deputy inspector, and captain.

5. This section provides a representative sample of the police densities of other major American municipal police departments. Police departments were selected because of a combination of city size and perceived professionalism/success. Table B-9, appendix B lists all other cities larger in population than Boston. See "Officers per 1000," [document on-line] available at http://www.policepay.net/officersper.asp; Internet; accessed 23 September 2005; and "2000 Census: US Municipalities Over 50,000: Ranked by 2000 Population," [document on-line] available at http://www.demographia.com/db-uscity98.htm; Internet; accessed 23 September 2005.

6. Originally, the Chicago Police Department subunits were called precincts as in New York. Before the 1960s, the Chicago Police Department had as many as 41 districts, which was eventually decreased to 21. With the advent of the 'community policing' approach to police work in the 1990s, the Chicago Police Department expanded its districts to the present 25. See "Brief History of the Chicago Police Department," *Chicago Historical Information*, August 1997 [document on-line] available at http://www.chipublib.org/004chicago/timeline/policedept.html; Internet; accessed 28 September 2005.

7. Chicago Police Department organization is listed in table B-10, appendix B. See *Chicago Police Department Annual Report: 2004 Year in Review*, [document on-line] available at http://egov.cityofchicago.org/webportal/COCWebPortal/COC_EDITORIAL/04AR.pdf; Internet; accessed 20 September 2005.

8. Philadelphia Police Department organization is outlined in table B-11, appendix B. See *Philadelphia Police Department 2003 Annual Report*, [document on-line] available at http://www.ppdonline.org/pdf/hq/Phila%20Police%20Annual%20lowres.pdf; Internet; accessed 22 September 2005; and the

Philadelphia Police Department website available at www.ppdonline.org, accessed 22 September 2005. Inspectors command patrol divisions, and captains command patrol districts. A patrol district is staffed by up to four platoons, each consisting of 1 lieutenant, 2 sergeants, and approximately 40 officers. Accordingly, districts range in size from about 100 to 160 officers.

9. *Philadelphia Police Department 2002 Annual Report*, 8 [document online] available at http://www.ppdonline.org/pdf/hq/2002report_low.pdf; Internet; accessed 19 September 2005.

10. The Boston Police Department is organized as follows:

Four Police Areas (A, B, C, D) and 11 Police Districts, the latter commanded by police captains. Districts are as follows:

- A-1 Downtown/Beacon Hill/Chinatown/Charlestown
- A-7 East Boston
- B-2 Roxbury/Mission Hill
- B-3 Mattapan/North Dorchester
- C-6 South Boston
- C-11 Dorchester
- D-4 Back Bay/Sound End/Fenway
- D-14 Allston/Brighton
- E-5 West Roxbury/Roslindale
- E-13 Jamaica Plain
- E-18 Hyde Park

The areas are insignificant organizationally and the districts each report directly to the police headquarters. The relatively small number of districts makes this a manageable structure. To add to the confusion of terminology in relation to other police departments, districts are also called patrol districts and were formerly known as divisions. See BPD website at http://www.cityofboston.gov/police/district.asp; Internet; accessed 30 August 2005; also Donna Wells, (Archivist, Boston Police Department) telephone interview by author, 20 September 2005.

11. Los Angeles had an ordinance limiting building height to 12 stories until 1966. See Daryl F. Gates with Diane K. Shah, *Chief: My Life in the L.A.P.D.* (New York: Bantam Books, 1992), 300.

12. Dave Krajicek, "The Crime Beat: LAPD Thumbnail, Ch. 1," *Covering Crime and Justice,* [document on-line] available at http://www.justicejournalism.org/crimeguide/chapter01/sidebars/chap01_resources.html; Internet; accessed 15 September 2005. Current figures vary slightly on the exact strength of the Los Angeles Police Department: from 9022 reported by Krajicek to 9241 found in the reference in note 24. The figure of 9195, between these two other figures, is cited at policepay.net, a website devoted to providing consult to police unions on pay issues. See http://www.policepay.net/zmainlinks/swornframe.htm; Internet; accessed 22 September 2005.

13. Table B-12, appendix B, shows the organization of the Los Angeles Police Department geographically and demographically.

14. As part of the LAPD's version of "community policing," since the mid-1970s, its patrol districts are now referred to as Basic Car Districts and several such districts under a sergeant as a Basic Car Area. See "Basic Car Plan," [document on-line] available at http://www.lapdonline.org/community/basic_car_plan/bcp.htm; Internet; accessed 14 September 2005 and Gates, 308.

15. The only comparable major cities with both a large population and a large land area are Houston, Texas, with an area of 540 square miles and a 1990 population of 1.6 million and San Diego, California, with an area of 324 square miles and a 1990 population of 1.1 million. However, the population densities of these two cities, 3000 and 3400 per square mile, respectively, are half the population density of Los Angeles. Proportionally, with a police force of 4786 officers, the Houston Police Department had a ratio of one police officer to every 334 residents, about 3 officers for every 1000 residents, and 8.9 police officers for every square mile of area. This places Houston roughly between the lower figures for Los Angeles and the higher figures for New York, Boston, Philadelphia, and Chicago. However, Houston's ratio of 8.9 officers per square miles is far lower than any other major city except San Diego, at half the area density of Los Angeles and only seven percent of New York. San Diego's 1190 police officers yield the astronomical ratios of 1 policeman for every 924 residents, about 1.1 (1.6 in relation to the current population) officers per 1000 city residents. This proportion is less than half of Los Angeles'. San Diego deploys 3.7 police officers per square mile of city area, proportionally equating to three percent of the force deployed by the New York Police Department. At least some of the reasoning behind the small size of the San Diego police force may be politically motivated. See "Thin Blue Line: San Diego needs more police," *San Diego Tribune* 12 December 2004 [article on-line] available at http://www.signonsandiego.com/uniontrib/20041212/news_1z1ed12top.html; Internet; accessed 16 September 2005; Campbell Gibson, "Population of the 100 Largest Cities and Other Urban Places in the United States: 1790 to 1990," (Washington, DC: US Census Bureau, June 1998) [document on-line] available at http://www.census.gov/population/www/documentation/twps0027.html#taba; Internet; accessed 16 September 2005.

16. Krajicek.

17. Gates, 59. A good discussion of the Los Angeles trolley system and its decline can be found at "The Red Cars of Los Angeles," *Los Angeles: Past, Present and Future*, 15 January 2002 [document on-line] available at http://www.usc.edu/isd/archives/la/historic/redcars/; Internet; accessed 22 September 2005.

18. See note 14 above.

19. LeSage.

20. Chicago Police Department, *Annual Report, 2004.*

21. Lieutenant Eamon McWilliams (Commander, Tow Squad/Fleet Liaison, Philadelphia Police Department) telephone interview by author, 22 September 2005. The Philadelphia Police Department deploys roughly 1000 marked and 500 unmarked patrol vehicles.

22. Boston Police Department. *Annual Report, 2003*; Wells.

23. See note 15.

24. *Los Angeles Police Department Plan of Action, Book II: For the LA that Could Be,* 11, 2004 [document on-line] available at http://www.lapdonline.org/pdf_files/poa/b2_plan.pdf; Internet; accessed 19 September 2005. Gates, 21, 105, 178, 203. According to Gates, the Los Angeles Police Department was 4300 strong in 1950 when Los Angeles had a population of 1.9 million, a proportion of one police officer for every 441 residents, or a ratio of 2.3 per 1000. In 1965 these ratios were 1 officer per 561 people and 1.91 officers per 1000 residents. By 1978, however, when Los Angeles' population was about 2.9 million, the proportions were 1 officer per 387 people and 2.6 officer per 1000 residents.

25. "Crime Rates for Selected Large Cities, 2002 (offenses known to the police per 100,000 inhabitants)," [document on-line] available at http://www.info please.com/ipa/A0004902.html; Internet; accessed 16 September 2005;"Table 1: Annual Estimates of the Population for Incorporated Places over 100,000, Ranked by July 1, 2004 Population: April 1, 2000 to July 1, 2004 (SUB-EST2004-01)," 2005, [spreadsheet on-line] available at http://www.census.gov/popest/cities/tables/SUB-EST2004-01.xls;Internet; accessed 22 September 2005. According to Gates, in 1991 Los Angeles ranked 35th in crime rates among major metropolitan areas. See Gates, 302. See *LAPD Annual Report 1996,* [document on-line] available at http://www.lapdonline.org/pdf_files/1996_annrprt.pdf; Internet; accessed 22 September 2005. This report stated crime rates had dropped over four consecutive years (1992-96) and during that same time period violent crime had dropped 11 percent and homicide, 34 percent. Despite the low crime rate ranking in 2002, LAPD publications cite a 10.4 percent increase in violent crime in Los Angeles between 1999 and 2002, making Los Angeles and Washington, DC, the only major US cities to show increases during the same period. See *LAPD Plan of Action: Book II,* 13.

26. Gates, 34, 302.

27. Ibid., 308; Ronald Oakerson and Shirley Svorny, "Rightsizing Los Angeles Government," *The Independent Review* 9, no. 4 (Spring 2005):513-528 [journal on-line] available at http://www.independent.org/pdf/tir/tir_09_4_3_oakerson.pdf; Internet; accessed 22 September 2005.

28. Gates, 303. Gates felt the criminal justice system, rather than the police themselves, were most responsible for increased crime rates towards the end of the century.

29. Ibid., 233; *LAPD Action Plan: Book II,* 14-15, 23.

30. The figure of 35 percent was derived arbitrarily, based on LAPD officials' perception of the professionalism of the force would allow it to "deliver sustainable low levels of crime in every Los Angeles neighborhood" with such an increase, even though the LAPD strength would still "remain well below those of most other large cities." See *LAPD Action Plan: Book II,* 23. The Los Angeles County voters defeated the sales tax increase on 3 November 2004.

31. *Los Angeles Police Department Plan of Action: Book I, LAPD Plan of Action, Book II: For the Los Angeles That Is,* 4, 2004 [document on-line] available at http://www.lapdonline.org/pdf_files/poa/b1_01_mandate.pdf; Internet;

accessed 22 September 2005. For an opinion from a Los Angeles resident and observer of public safety issues, see Russ Quan, "Los Angeles' Safer Communities Proposed Measure," *The Back Page*, 17 January 2005, http://nitewriter1. blogspot.com/2005_01_01_nitewriter1_archive.html; Internet; accessed 22 September 2005.

32. These figures use the projected size of the Los Angeles Police Department as even LAPD officials consider its current size inadequate.

33. Police force size figures are from the respective forces' public websites, their most recently available annual reports, and policepay.net.

34. Gary Cordner, "State Police in the United States-December 2003," [document on-line] available at http://www.csg.org/NR/rdonlyres/ex4lwhthmp cxm4pldsgebvlym4nlyprx4lg3wajkuzsoa4omqkxlt37bctcqp2kc7fdqr5qttjnu bt5gcuhr6mpknjb/State+Police+stats.pdf; Internet; accessed 26 August 2005; The New York State Police, with approximately 5000 members, is less than one-fifth the size of the New York Police Department. See the "Letter of Introduction," New York Division of State Police [document on-line] available at http://www. troopers.state.ny.us/introduction/; Internet; accessed 26 August 2005.

35. Benson, 187.

Chapter 4

Analysis

This work has reviewed historical case studies of successfully executed contingency operations and large police forces to provide a baseline and analytical data from which can be devised basic estimates for troop density. While formulating these estimates, the author recognizes each historical case study depicts a unique situation with its own specific set of factors contributing to the number of troops actually employed in the operation. In this section these factors will be analyzed along with a comparison of the various troop densities. As a starting point, troop density theory, as it currently exists, will be analyzed in relation to the statistics produced by this study.

Troop Density Theory

As mentioned in the introduction, since 1995 military observers, analysts, and civilian journalists have promulgated general theories on troop density. Most theorists to some extent cite historical precedent when proposing ratios for troop density levels. Most density recommendations fall within a range of 25 soldiers per 1000 residents in an area of operations (1 soldier per 40 inhabitants) to 20 soldiers per 1000 inhabitants (or 1 soldier per 50 inhabitants), while the lower figure of 20 to 1000 is considered the unofficial standard (or minimum requirement).[1]

A cursory look at the statistics (figures 19 and 20) from the case studies of successful past contingency operations shows that, with the exception of the Kosovo peacekeeping operation, none of the operations studied here come close to the recommended ratios of 20 soldiers to 1000 population or 1 troop to 50 population.

These numbers, while based on maximum deployment strengths, do not include totals for indigenous troops, local police forces, or contractor support. This point will be discussed and analyzed separately. Occupation force size planning estimates are also included in the graphs where available. These graphs also visually illustrate the lack of a standard for determining troop density as well as the haphazard nature of these estimates in which some operations had a greater number of troops actually deployed and others had fewer.

Between 1941 and 1997, the US Army produced, and periodically updated, a manual of historically based planning factors, FM 101-10-1/2, *Staff Officers' Field Manual: Organizational, Technical, and Logistical Data Planning Factors*. This comprehensive compendium of tables and

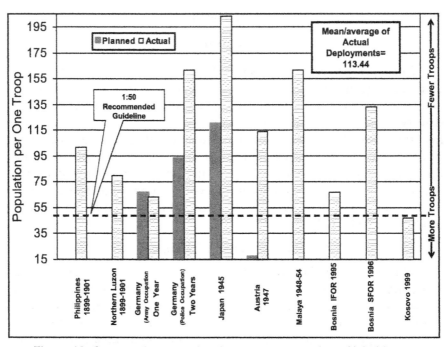

Figure 19. Comparative troop density: troops per number of inhabitants.

charts was last updated in 1990 and discarded in 1996. While the manual contains detailed tables covering planning factors for support of various operations, the focus is clearly logistics and not operations. For example, the personnel section contains planning factors for projecting casualties and providing replacements. However, it does not provide any general planning guidance on how large the force should be for different types of operations relative to the opposing enemy force size, the geographic size of the area of operations or, in the case of a contingency operation, the size, and density of the local population. In a telling passage at the beginning of the personnel section, the planner is clearly advised he will be working within the parameters of an already specified force size, in which the "…planning normally conforms to the personnel strength ceiling authorized by the theater and subordinate commands."[2] Unfortunately, no US Army document provides specific operational planning factors and guidance equivalent to the combat service support guidance in FM 101-10-1/2. The rationale behind this may be alluded to in the following excerpt from that manual:

> Troop basis planning is not absolutely predictable. Planners must consider an infinite variety of operational

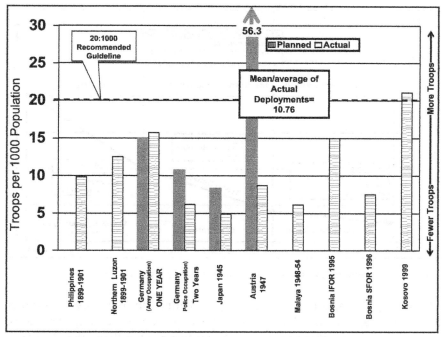

Figure 20. Comparative troop density per 1000 population.

environments and the vital role of human factors, which
may complicate analysis and/or their justification.[3]

Accordingly, except for general operational planning concepts and
guidance, the US Army provides no guidance or planning factors to use
when planning the size of a force to engage in contingency operations. In
addition, during the post-Cold War era, the logistic planning factors were
also discarded.[4] The US Army historically has not and currently does not
provide specific planning information for troop levels in various types of
operations. The Army has probably done this deliberately in line with the
old dictum everything in combat "depends on the situation."[5]

While the Army has not provided any extensive theory on troop density, civilian defense analysts have. Rand Corporation mathematician and
military analyst, James Quinlivan, promulgates the most comprehensive
theory. Quinlivan espouses a spectrum, or sliding scale, of troop density
in contingency operations.

In his model, Quinlivan classifies operations into three levels of intensity. As the intensity of the operation increases, the size of the force proportionally increases. (Quinlivan uses the term stability operation instead

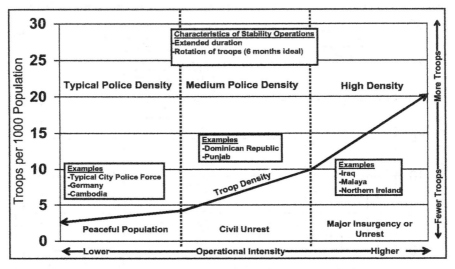

Figure 21. James Quinlivan's model of troop density.

of contingency operation.) According to Quinlivan, typically operations at all levels are of extended duration and are executed by troops and units rotating in and out of the operation. According to Quinlivan, the ideal tour length is six months. The highest level, major insurgency or unrest, requires a minimum troop density of 20 troops to 1000 population, a figure, as mentioned above, usually cited as the standard level for all contingency operations, including Quinlivan when he discusses the operations in Iraq. Quinlivan's model is depicted in figure 21.[6]

While Quinlivan posits an interesting model for troop density, a critical analysis of his work identifies several points of concern. First, many of the numbers Quinlivan uses in his examples are higher than numbers used in this study for the same operations. Second, he inconsistently includes indigenous forces in his accounting of the total number of troops deployed in support of specific operations. For example, in Quinlivan's analysis of the Malaya Emergency, he correctly cites early 1952 as the apex of British troop deployment in that operation. He rightfully cites a force of 30 battalions and an overall troop strength of 40,000. However, most sources place this number closer to 30,000.[7]

To reach the ratio of 20 troops to 1000 inhabitants, Quinlivan then includes the 71,000 members of various Malay police and home defense forces in his calculations. Therefore, he tacitly equates all types of forces as equal in terms of troop density, this in spite of contemporary British insistence that police forces were no substitute for soldiers in counterinsurgency operations.[8] Despite the British reluctance to equate indigenous forces with their own operational military forces, it will be discussed here that Quinlivan was right to include them. However, in later versions of his theory, Quinlivan includes only "international forces."[9] Troop density figures from the various case studies will be shown to vary far less when operational indigenous or other forces are included.

Quinlivan's theory provides a good analysis, particularly his scale of intensity levels of the operations as it relates to troop density. However, while Quinlivan places most of the operations in the mid- to high-intensity level, the figures produced in this work will place most operations in the low- to mid-intensity level. This implies his ratio of 20:1000 is too high a benchmark for troop density in contingency operations.[10]

A final analysis of troop density theory is found in another Rand study, *America's Role in Nation-Building: From Germany to Iraq*, completed by James Dobbins and his team in 2003. While the focus of Dobbins' study is nation building not troop density, its compilation of troop densities for past examples of contingency operations reflects the troop levels found in this study rather than those found in Quinlivan's.[11] While Dobbins' team did not prescribe any specific troop density levels, they did observe higher troop densities resulted in decreased friendly and hostile casualties, meaning the greater the proportion of troops used in an operation, the less intense the resistance.[12]

Factors Affecting Troop Density

Ideally, the troop densities in figures 19 and 20 would be identical or close to the same proportional level. However, as can be seen in figure 22, this is not the case. Figure 22 depicts how the various case studies are grouped around the mean or average. The average troop density of the various case studies in this work is 10.76 soldiers per 1000 of population (or 113.44 residents per soldier). The disparity in density among the examples is 16.20 soldiers per 1000 residents from the least dense operation (Japan) and the densest operation (Kosovo).

What caused such a wide spread? There must be mitigating factors. Each historical example has specific factors possibly affecting the actual troop density for the operation. Therefore, a brief review of these factors is now in order. These factors are interconnected and can have a modifying effect on troop density, requiring greater or lesser densities. The following analysis of troop density factors is based on the maximum number of troops deployed for the contingency operation, as are all troop density statistics in this work.

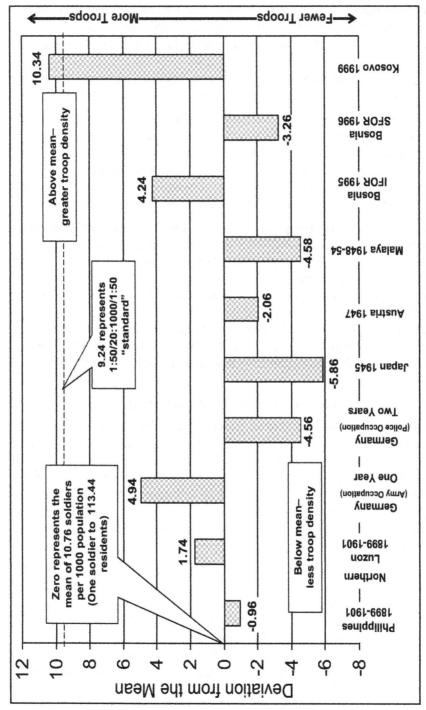

Figure 22. Troop density variations of selective troop deployments.

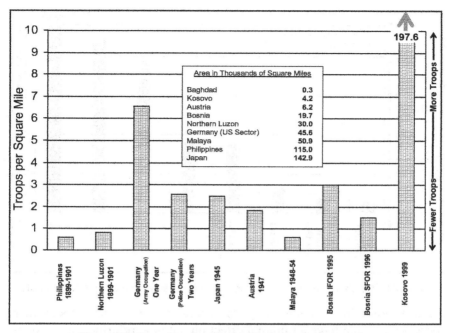

Figure 23. Area density of selective troop deployments.

Area

As illustrated in figure 23, the size of the area into which the troops deploy seemingly has no actual impact on troop density. That planners based troop deployments in contingency operations primarily on population density rather than patrol area is a point this work has discussed previously, particularly relating to the Germany case study. In addition, as discussed here, the size, organization, and structure of police forces are based primarily on population rather than area.

A key issue to consider when planning for troop density is the density of the local population in relation to the geographic area. In such instances, where the geographic area is small, the soldier to area ratio and soldier to population ratio will be disproportionally high, even if a small force is employed. Kosovo and Bosnia are good examples of this. In such areas, fewer forces provided high troop densities. In this respect, the relatively small size of the operational area clearly affects the troop density.

This factor should also be called the "sense of proportion" factor. In a smaller contingency operation, deploying a higher proportion of troops can still yield a relatively small total force package. The extra number of troops remains minimal enough not to have a major effect on national

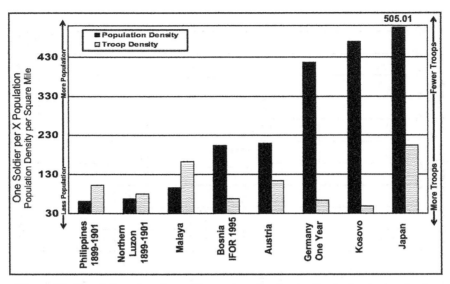

Figure 24. Population density and troop density of selective troop deployments.

security elsewhere. Accordingly, the cautious use of more troops than necessary would have a minimal effect on national priorities or missions elsewhere. This provides smaller deployments with a margin for error in terms of appropriate troop density unavailable in larger deployments. **Therefore, density figures from small deployments should be taken with a grain of salt, particularly if their sums are disproportionately higher than average densities of larger historical deployments.**

Population Density

Figure 24 shows comparative figures relating population density to troop density. This work has already established that troop densities are based on population. However, there appears to be no readily discernible correlation between population density and troop density. Contingency operations with similar population densities, for example Austria in 1947 and Kosovo in 1999, do not have the same troop density. While Japan had the second highest population density in this study, its troop density was proportionally the lowest. While population density is a key factor in determining the number of troops used in a contingency operation, there must be other mitigating factors affecting the actual density of the troops in proportion to the population.

Troops Available

The overall availability of troops is a factor in determining troop density. Following the defeat of a conventional force, it is likely there would be a large number of troops available for occupation duty. Conversely, successful campaigns conducted as economy of force operations may result in a shortage of troops for follow-on contingency missions. Operations where there were a large number of available troops at the start include the occupations of Germany and Japan at the end of World War II, Malaya, and the peacekeeping missions in Bosnia and Kosovo in the 1990s. In Malaya, the British had recently shifted a number of Gurkha units formerly stationed in India to Malaya. The Malayan example is a special case because the British command required even more forces as the operation continued. Otherwise, in most such cases, troop density is greatest early in the operation. The operations in the Balkans clearly show the relationship of a dense area to the troops available. For example, in Kosovo, the US Army was able to deploy the equivalent of a brigade-size force and still obtain the very high troop density level of 21.1 troops per 1000 of population while actually utilizing a relatively small force.

Inversely, there have been operations, such as those in the Philippines in 1899, where there was an initial shortage of troops because the preceding campaign required fewer troops than the subsequent contingency operation.[13] In such operations, additional troops not involved in the original operation were deployed to provide a larger force. In the case of the Philippine Insurrection, the troops used initially had been raised to fight in the War with Spain, but fought Filipino insurgents instead. When the term of service of the war volunteers expired, national volunteer troops recruited specifically for use in the Insurrection replaced them. When the term of service of the national volunteers expired, regular troops, in turn, replaced them. The regular troop allotment had been increased specifically to meet the requirements in the Philippines. Even in campaigns with an initial dearth of troops, certain areas may have more troops available than other areas because of the way the campaign ended and where the troops were when it ended. For example, in the Philippines, the initial deployment of troops centered on Manila and central Luzon because the force was deployed to secure Manila.

Troop Rotation

A factor closely related to available troops is troop rotation. If the expected duration of the operation is long, units and individuals may rotate through the mission. The effect of an individual rotation plan on an army which rotates its soldiers as individuals has little affect on troop density. For example, the US Army troops rotations in Germany, Austria, and Japan provide a good example of this. However, for a force conducting a contingency operation with rotating units, the total number of available units across the total force could affect the number of units actually deployed at one time (i.e. an equal force would have to be available to replace the deployed troops). Additionally, the lack of continuity inherent in unit rotations could affect the success of the operation. Sometimes unit rotations can be unplanned, as with the US forces in the Philippines where personnel turned over twice during the Insurrection, and where the final replacements were long-serving regular troops whose numbers were increased just for their role in the Philippines. In Malaya the British employed a combination of unit rotation and long-serving troops. While British battalions and those from most other Commonwealth nations rotated on average every one to three years using soldiers on short enlistments or draftees, Gurkha and Malay battalions were basically in-country for the duration of the conflict, simultaneously providing the British forces with a combination of fresh troops and experienced troops.[14]

Troops Recruited

Another factor related to troop availability and rotation is troop recruitment. While most contingency operations use troops already available, in some cases, forces were recruited specifically for the contingency mission. As previously stated, the best example of this is the Philippines Insurrection where 24 regiments of national volunteer troops were raised specifically for duty in the islands. Additionally, the Regular Army was expanded several times during the period, the last time to replace the departing volunteers upon the expiration of their terms of service.

Similarly, during the Malayan Emergency, the British government enacted a conscription system called National Service to provide adequate personnel to meet the military needs of the postwar era. While this draft was not adopted specifically for service in Malaya, the forces in Malaya were ultimately composed of a large number of National Servicemen.

Troops recruited specifically for an operation may not provide operational continuity, adversely affecting the outcome of the contingency operation. In the operations studied in this work, a combination of troop rotation overlaps, recruitment of veteran troops, and a combination of rotating new troops and retaining longer serving veteran troops minimized the affect of a lack of continuity.

Duration/Intensity

Apart from personnel, demographic, and geographic factors, the nature of the operation itself is an important consideration. While every contingency operation studied in this work lasted at least several years, only certain operations retained a high level of intensity for most of the duration.

For example, both the Philippines Insurrection and the Malayan Emergency were counterinsurgency operations rather than peacekeeping or occupation missions. Troop density in such intense operations often is at its maximum not at the start of the operation, but at some point in the middle, often about the time the tide turns against the insurgents.

Substitute Forces

In most cases, military forces, including support troops, are composed of regular serving troops. However, there is precedent for the use of substitute forces such as Gurkha troops in Malaya. At any given time, the British forces included up to eight battalions of Gurkha personnel recruited from **Nepal to fight for the British crown. These forces deployed in convention**ally organized military units and served under the British command. Gurkha **troop numbers are included in British and Commonwealth strength figures** for the Malaya campaign. Apart from the Gurkhas, the most common use of substitute forces is the employment of civilian contractors. While the use of **such contractors was not significant in the case studies analyzed here, they** will be discussed later in this work in relation to the operation in Iraq.

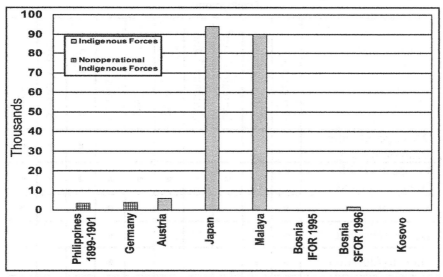

Figure 25. Available indigenous forces in selective troop deployments.

Indigenous Forces

In addition to contractors, the availability of any operational indigenous forces (army or police) would naturally affect the number and density of troops employed for a contingency operation.[15] (See figure 25 for numbers of indigenous forces deployed in the selected case studies.) While local forces were present in almost every operation studied in this work, many of these forces were not yet capable of taking over responsibilities from the deployed forces (Philippines and Germany,) or were unemployable because they were hostile threats either to the occupiers or to rival forces (Bosnia and Kosovo). In three cases (Austria, Japan, and Malaya), there was a sizeable indigenous police force in place at the height of troop deployment.[16].

Review of Factors

Table 9 lists the factors affecting troop density by each case study.[17] The last row of the table compares the table with the values expressed in figure 22, i.e. whether the particular operation was above (less troop density) or below (higher troop density) the mean troop density values of all the studied operations.

As the information in the table demonstrates, the one common factor in all the less dense (above the mean) troop deployments was the presence of operational substitute or indigenous forces. This would seem to indicate that

Table 9. Comparison of Factors Affecting Troop Density in Selective Troop Deployments

	Philippines	Northern Luzon	Germany 1 year	Germany 2 year	Japan	Austria	Malaya	Bosnia IFOR	Bosnia SFOR	Kosovo
Dense geographic area/pop density								●	●	●
Troops available/ initially on hand			●		●	●	●	●	●	●
Troop rotation	●	●					●	●		●
Troops recruited	●	●					●			
Intensity/duration	●	●					●			
Substitute forces							●			
Indigenous forces			●	●	●	●			●	
Troop density (+/- mean) + = more troops — = less troops	—	+	+	—	—	—	—	+	—	+

102

planners and commanders of the deployed force included the availability of such forces when determining the number of troops required. Figure 26 is a revised version of figure 22. The adjusted number of troops deployed derives from the inclusion of the number of operational indigenous or substitute forces (including police) into the total number of troops counted at the time of maximum deployment. [18] The inclusion of available operational substitute and indigenous forces adjusts the mean troop density from the selected case studies in this work adjusts to a figure of 13.26 soldiers per 1000 inhabitants or 91.82 inhabitants per soldier.

The data displayed in figure 26 shows that when the adjusted figures are considered, the least dense contingency operations are Japan and Germany during the Constabulary era, and the densest operation is the Malayan Emergency. Using personnel numbers as a baseline for troop density, the mean figure of 13.26 soldiers per 1000 of population (or 1 soldier per 91.82 inhabitants) provides a good raw planning factor. All of the adjusted densities fall within a range of plus or minus 18.60 soldiers per 1000 of population, as depicted by the darker bars in figure 26. As it relates to the factors previously discussed, this variation, equal to a range of between 7 and 25 soldiers per 1000 of population (or 41 and 161 residents per 1 soldier), is illustrated in table 10.

An analysis of the factors in relation to the relative troop density of specific operations depicts no glaring patterns to account for the disparity of troop density levels. With the exception of Malaya, high intensity operations over extended periods of time tend to be grouped around the mean value, while operations where more troops were available tend to also employ proportionally more troops. Such variations likely reflect a combination of the unique qualities of each operation and the "fog of war," i.e. deployment sizes based on an unknown situation. This variance can also be seen in the planning for these operations.

Gulf Between Planning and Execution

Figure 19 represented the difference between planning estimates and the number of troops actually deployed in support of a specific operation. Table 11 illustrates the difference between the planning estimates and actual troop deployments in the operations for which planning figures are available. Again, the numbers show no discernible pattern. In three of the four cases, troop numbers were overestimated. Two factors account for the differences between planning estimates and the actual number deployed in both Austria and Japan. First planners feared significant resistance that never materialized, and second a sizeable force was available to execute the operations.

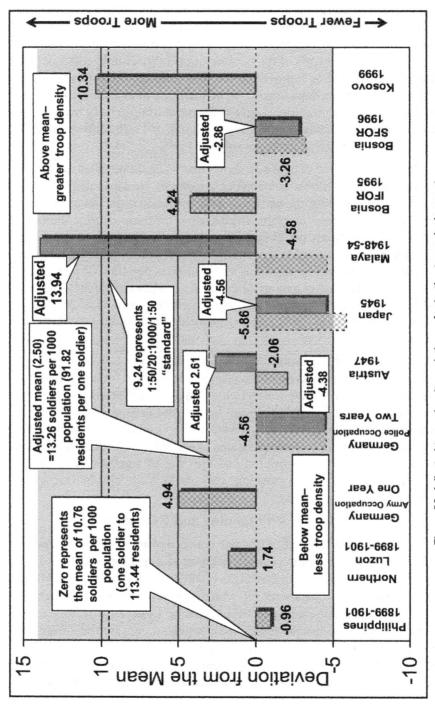

Figure 26. Adjusted troop density variations of selective troop deployments.

104

Table 10. Troop Density Variation in Terms of Key Factors

		Troop Density (+/- adjusted mean of 13.26 soldiers per 1000 population)	Dense Area	Troops Available	Troop Rotation	Troops Recruited	Intensity/ Duration	Substitute Forces	Indigenous forces
Malaya		11.44		●	●	●	●	●	●
Kosovo	More	7.84	●		●				
Germany 1 year		2.44		●					
Bosnia IFOR	Troops	1.74	●	●	●				
Austria		0.11		●					●
Northern Luzon		-0.76			●	●	●		
Philippines		-3.46			●	●	●		
Bosnia SFOR	Fewer	-5.36	●	●	●				●
Germany 2 years		-6.88							●
Japan		-7.06		●					●

Table 11. Planning Versus Execution

Operation	Planned Size (troops per 1000 pop)	Actual Size (troops per 1000 pop)	Difference (planned vs. actual) (troops per 1000 pop)
Germany 1 year	15	16	+1.0
Germany 2 years	11	6.2	-4.8
Austria	56.3	11	-45.3
Japan	8.3	4.9	-3.4

Raw Troop Density Size Conclusions

Based on the above analysis, this work proposes the figure of 13.26 soldiers per 1000 inhabitants or 91.82 residents per soldier as a basic planning factor for determining troop density in contingency operations. This recommendation comes with the caveat that any variations in troop density are because of specific issues arising from each situation. This planning estimate includes numbers of all available operational indigenous and substitute (contractor/mercenary) forces, as well as deployed soldiers.

Organization and Troop Density in Contingency Operations

The previous discussion concerns basic numbers of troops. However, types of forces to be deployed are key to any analysis of troop density. Planners do not plan using just numbers of soldiers but also the need for specific types of military units. The major two categories considered are police-style forces and operational forces.

Police Forces

This work contains a detailed discussion of police density in various cities. From this analysis, clearly even the police density of a city like New York, with its ratio of 204.8 residents per police officer (4.9 officers per 1000 of population), is considerably smaller than the proportion deployed in most contingency operations. However, the average police density of 248.12 residents per police officer (4.1 officers per 1000 of population) employed by the most successful major municipal police departments in the United States for daily operations leads to the conclusion that forces executing a contingency operation need to dedicate a proportion of their force equal to the above ratios specifically to police duties. Therefore, of the recommended planning figure of 13.26 soldiers per 1000 of population planning figure, at least 4.1 (30 percent or almost one-third of the force) should be devoted specifically to police duties.

Operational Forces

Pundits and other observers often ignore the fact that military forces do not determine their troop densities based on numbers of individual troops, but rather on the number of operational units needed to accomplish the mission. (Table 12 details operational forces deployed in contingency operations.) Based on the scope of the contingency operation and the army's organization, divisions were used in Germany, Japan, and Austria as the operational unit, brigades and regiments in Kosovo, Bosnia, and the Philippines, and battalions in Malaya. The number of headquarters and support troops would then be devised based on how

Table 12. Operational Forces in Contingency Operations

	(a) Brigade Equivalent Size	(b) Maximum No. of Brigade Equivalents (actual brigades deployed)	(c) Maximum No. of Bde Equivalent Total Force (actual brigades plus other operational forces)	(d) Population Density/ Bde (pop/b)	(e) Population Density/ Bde/ Total Force (pop/c)	(f) Area Density/Bde (square mile) (actual brigades deployed) (area/b)	(g) Area Density/Bde (square mile) (total force deployed) (area/c)
Philippines	3583	19.20	19.20	368,421	368,421	5990	5990
Germany 1 year	11,971	25.00	25.00	760,000	760,000	1824	1824
Austria	5673	2.00	3.00	648,850	432,567	3100	2066
Japan	7389	48.00	60.72	1,503,063	1,188,192	2977	2353
Malaya	3000	10.00	40.00	485,600	121,400	5085	1271
Bosnia IFOR	6000	10.00	10.00	400,000	400,000	1974	1974
Kosovo	8324	5.00	5.00	394,000	394,000	841	841
Police Forces	1333			200,550	200,550		
Average	5909			595,061	483,141	3113	2706

many operational units they would be expected to command or support. The US Army's reorganization into the modular Army structure in the early 21st century is, in fact, an attempt to create more operational units (brigades). Civil municipal police forces, also organized by operational units, deploy based on the area and the population they support.

Using the operations studied in this work, deployed operational forces have been divided into brigade equivalents; their individual force numbers and proportions are determined based on population and area. Including police department organization, the average size of the brigade-equivalent element in organizations for the operations featured in this work is 5909 (column a, table 12). This sum includes support troops, headquarters troops and an equal slice of all separate elements not assigned to any brigade. The average population density per brigade is one brigade for every 595,061 inhabitants (column d). These figures do not include any indigenous or substitute forces operationally deployed. If substitute and indigenous forces are included, the average population density per brigade equivalent is 483,141 (column e).

Operationally, deployed forces typically set up a number of bases. The troop density of bases could also be a key factor in overall troop density. However, further research on base distribution will be required to determine planning estimates for this dimension of troop density. The only available figures are those from the Bosnia operation, in which there were 536.34 soldiers per base camp. Given the brigade-equivalent size of 6000 for Bosnia, this equates to a rough estimate of 12 base camps per brigade equivalent, but this figure cannot be extrapolated across all operations because it is based solely on the experience in Bosnia.

Summary

The general planning figures for troop density as determined in this work are in table 13. These are general guidelines based on the mean from past military operations. Each operation will have its own unique circumstances and situational factors requiring adjustments to the planning figures. Nevertheless, as recommended here, these historically based guidelines will be useful as planning factors for future operations.

These planning figures do not include the ongoing operation in Iraq. In the next chapter, the Iraq operation will be analyzed using the same criteria as the previous case studies and then will be compared to the above planning factors to determine how it relates to those factors.

Table 13. Troop Density Planning Factors

Troop Density: (including indigenous forces and substitute forces)	13.26 soldiers per 1000 91.82 inhabitants per soldier
Proportion of Troop Density Devoted to Police Operations	4.1 per thousand/ 30 percent of force size
Brigade-equivalent Size (including support slice):	5909
Brigade Equivalent to Population Ratio	One brigade per 483,141 inhabitants

Notes

1.   Stephen Budiansky, "Formula for How Many Troops We Need," *Washington Post,* 9 May 2004, p. B04 [article on-line] available at http://www.spokes manreview.com/breaking-news-story.asp?submitdate=2004510151143; Internet; accessed 13 January 2005; Daniel Smith, "Iraq: Descending into the Quagmire," *Foreign Policy In Focus Policy Report,* June 2003 [document on-line] available at http://www.fpif.org/papers/quagmire2003.html; Internet; accessed 9 November 2005; Kevin Drum, "Political Animal: Not Enough Troops in Iraq?" *Washington Monthly,* 9 January 2005 [article on-line] available at http://www.washing tonmonthly.com/archives/individual/2005_01/005422.php; Internet; accessed 14 January 2005; James Quinlivan, "Burden of Victory: The Painful Arithmetic of Stability Operations," *Rand Review,* 27 no. 3 (Summer 2003) 18 August 2005 [article on-line] available at http://www.rand.org/publications/randreview/issues/ summer2003/burden.html; Internet; accessed 14 September 2005; James Quinlivan, "Force Requirements in Stability Operations," *Parameters,* 23 (Winter 1995) : 59-69.

2.   FM 101-10-1/2, *Staff Officers' Field Manual: Organizations, Technical, and Logistical Data Planning Factors* vol. 2, change 1 (Washington, DC: Department of the Army, 17 July 1990), p. 6-0.

3.   Ibid.

4.   FM 101-10-1/2 was formally rescinded by the October 1997 edition *of Department of the Army Pamphlet (DA PAM) 25-30, Consolidated Index of Army Publications and Blank Forms.*

5.   Army publications relating to contingency operations, including *Interim FM 3-07.22, Counterinsurgency Operations* issued in 2004, and *FM 100-23, Peace Operations,* published in 1994, only address troop density in very general terms.

6.   Quinlivan, "Burden of Victory"; Quinlivan, "Force Requirements in Stability Operations." See note 1 for references to sources which use the 20:1000 as the standard level for troop density. In "Burden for Victory," Quinlivan seemingly contradicts both his previous writings and his own comments earlier in the same article when he codifies the 20:1000 ratio as only including "foreign troops" when discussing the Iraqi operation and in a figure accompanying the article, which applies the same standard to various other recent operations as well as Iraq.

7.   Quinlivan, "Force Requirements in Stability Operations"; Jackson, 18-9; Coates, 168. Quinlivan's population estimate for Malaya is about 700,000 higher than the figure used in this work, probably due to a 1948 figure used here [this work uses population estimates from the beginning of operations] and a 1952 figure used by Quinlivan.

8.   Scurr, 6; Jackson, 17-8; Coates, 92, 123, 165.

9.   See note 6 for further discussion of this point.

10.   Using Quinlivan's Malay methodology and adding the 124,000 members of the Iraqi security forces to the 184,500 deployed Coalition troops in January 2005 yields a ratio of 12:1000, still far below the 20:2000 level, while, however,

just surpassing Quinlivan's threshold of 10:2000 separating his mid- from high-intensity troop density requirement categories.

11. Dobbins et al., 150-1.

12. Ibid., 153.

13. The 2003 Baghdad campaign is another example.

14. While Quinlivan considers six-month troop rotations to be ideal, there are very few such short rotations utilized in the case studies examined in this work. The Kosovo peacekeeping operation has been a six-month rotation and some nations used shorter rotations in Bosnia. But in Malaya, British forces deployed for two to three years, and US Army forces in Iraq have been on one year rotations, although US Marine forces and coalition troops have rotated in shorter intervals. In the case of the Marines, a seven-month rotation is used, but Marine troops are eligible for another tour after seven months out of Iraq, while Army policy is a minimum of one year between Iraqi rotations.

15. Especially in counterinsurgency operations, local forces are of particular importance to successful operations. See John A. Nagl, *Learning to Eat Soup with a Knife: Counterinsurgency Lessons from Malaya and Vietnam*, revised edition (Chicago: University of Chicago Press, 2005), xiv-xv.

16. In Kosovo during the SFOR deployment, a small international police force was organized.

17. Definitions of the categories used in the table can be found on page 111.

18. This chart is based on the raw data found in the table in appendix A, where it is listed as adjusted in the first column.

• Indicates factor was present in operation.	
Dense Geographical Area/ Population Density	A compact geographical area with a high population density.
Troops Available/Initially On Hand	A large number of troops available at the start of the operation.
Troop Rotation	Troops rotated through the operation as units.
Troops Recruited	Troops were recruited specifically for participation in the operation.
Intensity/Duration	Throughout most of its duration the operation continued at a high operational intensity level.
Substitute Forces	Mercenary (i.e. Gurkha) or civilian contractor forces were employed as operational substitutes for regular forces.
Indigenous Forces	Locally recruited forces or international police forces were operationally employed.

Chapter 5

Iraq 2003-05

Situational Narrative

The contingency operation following the March-April 2003 Baghdad campaign continued through October 2005 while troop numbers remained at relatively the same level as at the start of the operation. However, there had been indications the first major operational downsizing would soon occur, as Iraqi forces replaced American and Coalition forces in certain areas and contexts.[1] Since July 2003, the on-the-ground troop strength of Coalition forces in Iraq has remained at roughly 176,000, as US force numbers fluctuated between 108,000 and 160,000.[2]

Similar to the Philippine Insurrection and the Malayan Emergency, forces used in the contingency operation exceeded the numbers required for the preceding conventional operations. In the case of the Iraq operation, those forces originally earmarked for the conventional campaign that had not arrived in Iraq at the time of Baghdad campaign, served as occupation forces.

Between April and July 2003, occupation forces were deployed as illustrated in figure 27. Originally, Marine forces, the entire 3d Infantry Division (Mechanized), and the 101st Airborne Division (Air Assault) patrolled the precincts of Baghdad. The 101st was soon shifted to northern Iraq to the vicinity of Mosul. The Marines took over a sector in south-central Iraq that included the cities of Najaf and Nasiriyah, while the 1st Armored Division deployed to the theater and assumed responsibility for the Baghdad area from the 3d Infantry Division. The 3d Infantry division then was shifted west to Anbar Province, an area originally allocated only a single brigade-size armored cavalry regiment. Anbar, while mostly uninhabited desert, contained the restive Sunni Arab cities of Ramadi and Fallujah, requiring a larger force than originally estimated. The British 1st Armoured Division was deployed in the south around the city of Basra.

The shape of a more permanent occupation force began to develop in July 2003 when multinational forces began deploying to Iraq to augment or replace American and British forces. The largest contingents were from Poland, the Ukraine, Spain, and Italy. The higher commands for the occupation evolved as well. In May civilian government functions had been delegated to a new agency, the Coalition Provisional Authority (CPA), under retired ambassador L. Paul Bremer. Bremer reported directly to the US Secretary of Defense. Militarily, the Baghdad campaign had

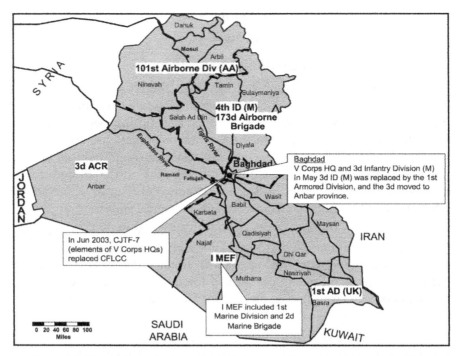

Figure 27. Troop dispositions in the initial occupation of Iraq, May-July 2003.

been fought under the control of the Combined Forces Land Component Command (CFLCC). Under CFLCC were two major subordinate corps-size commands, V Corps and I Marine Expeditionary Force (I MEF). To manage the military aspects of the occupation, CFLCC was replaced by Combined Joint Task Force-7 (CJTF-7), a headquarters formed from the V Corps staff. I MEF redeployed out of Iraq in the fall of 2003.

Four regionally-based division sectors were organized under CJTF-7: two under American control, one in the north-central area and one in Baghdad, one under Polish command south of Baghdad, and one under British command in the extreme south. An additional US division-size force would subsequently be deployed to Anbar Province.[3] Immediately following the fall of Baghdad, an American division operated in the north-western region around the city of Mosul. The division was replaced by a brigade in 2004, and in 2005 a division-size force was returned to the northwestern sector. Each division or force was responsible for a distinct sector, although during the Shiite uprising in 2004, the boundaries would temporarily be redrawn to allow large number of US forces to be intro-duced into what had been the Polish sector in the cities of Karbala, Najaf, and Kut, for the duration of that operation.[4] Otherwise, sectors were generally divided by Iraqi provinces.

Within the first year of the occupation, all Coalition forces began troop rotations generally six months in duration for non-American forces and a year or slightly longer for US Army forces.[5] The first group of forces in Iraq were designated as Operation IRAQI FREEDOM-I (OIF -I). The OIF-I forces rotated out of the theater in a staggered manner. The Marines and the 3d Infantry Division (Mechanized) that had done most of the fighting in the Baghdad campaign redeployed first in the fall of 2003. A majority of the remaining OIF-I forces redeployed in the early spring of 2004, although the Shiite uprising in Najaf in April 2004 resulted in the 1st Armored Division remaining in the country several months beyond its original redeployment date.

OIF-II began when the I MEF replaced the 82d Airborne Division as Multinational Forces-West (MNF-W) in March 2004 in Anbar Province. The last OIF-I unit, the 1st Armored Division, redeployed in July 2004 ending OIF-I.[6] In May 2004 as part of the OIF-II transition, the land component headquarters, CJTF-7, was replaced by two new commands, a theater command called Multinational Forces-Iraq (MNF-I) and an operational command called Multinational Corps-Iraq (MNC-I). MNF-I was a composite command, designed to interface with the new Iraqi provisional government, which would assume governance responsibilities in Iraq from the CPA in July 2004. MNC-I was a placeholder command staffed by rotating US corps headquarters. The III Corps headquarters deployed from Fort Hood, Texas, to command MNC-I during OIF-II.

During the OIF-II rotation, there was also a large-scale introduction of reserve component ground combat units into the occupation order of battle, as brigades from the Arkansas, Oregon, and North Carolina Army National Guard were deployed into Iraq and integrated into active Army divisions. While most elements were replaced by like-size units, in northwestern Iraq around the city of Mosul, a brigade equipped with the Stryker, the recently fielded, eight-wheeled, armored combat vehicle, replaced the 101st Airborne Division (Air Assault).[7]

The transfer of authority from OIF-I to OIF-II was originally intended to mark the first programmed reduction in the number of US troops from approximately 141,900 to about 100,000. In February 2004 US troop numbers did slightly decrease to 108,000 because of troop deployments and redeployments in theater, however, this was only a temporary reduction. By April 2004 troop numbers increased to more

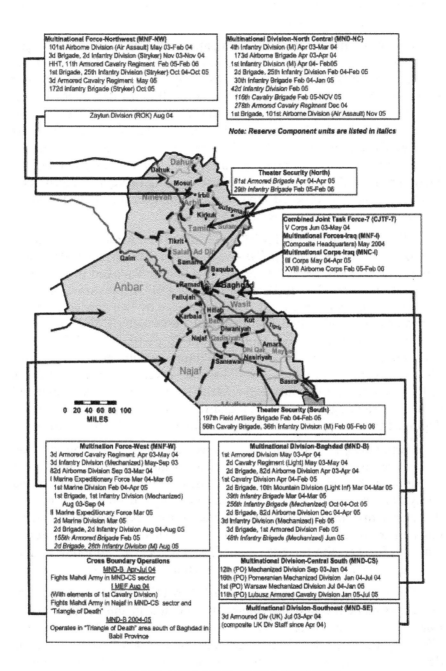

Multinational Force-Northwest (MNF-NW)
101st Airborne Division (Air Assault) May 03-Feb 04
3d Brigade, 2d Infantry Division (Stryker) Nov 03-Nov 04
HHT, 11th Armored Cavalry Regiment Feb 06-Feb 06
1st Brigade, 25th Infantry Division (Stryker) Oct 04-Oct 05
3d Armored Cavalry Regiment May 05
172d Infantry Brigade (Stryker) Oct 05

Zaytun Division (ROK) Aug 04

Multinational Division-North Central (MND-NC)
4th Infantry Division (M) Apr 03-Mar 04
173d Airborne Brigade Apr 03-Apr 04
1st Infantry Division (M) Apr 04- Feb05
2d Brigade, 25th Infantry Division Feb 04-Feb 05
30th Infantry Brigade Feb 04-Jan 05
42d Infantry Division Feb 05
116th Cavalry Brigade Feb 05-NOV 05
278th Armored Cavalry Regiment Dec 04
1st Brigade, 101st Airborne Division (Air Assault) Nov 05

Note: Reserve Component units are listed in italics

Theater Security (North)
81st Armored Brigade Apr 04-Apr 05
29th Infantry Brigade Feb 05-Feb 06

Combined Joint Task Force-7 (CJTF-7)
V Corps Jun 03-May 04
Multinational Forces-Iraq (MNF-I)
(Composite Headquarters) May 2004
Multinational Corps-Iraq (MNC-I)
III Corps May 04-Apr 05
XVIII Airborne Corps Feb 05-Feb 06

Theater Security (South)
197th Field Artillery Brigade Feb 04-Feb 05
56th Cavalry Brigade, 36th Infantry Division (M) Feb 05-Feb 06

Multination Force-West (MNF-W)
3d Armored Cavalry Regiment Apr 03-May 04
3d Infantry Division (Mechanized) May-Sep 03
82d Airborne Division Sep 03-Mar 04
I Marine Expeditionary Force Mar 04-Mar 05
  1st Marine Division Feb 04-Apr 05
  1st Brigade, 1st Infantry Division (Mechanized)
    Aug 03-Sep 04
II Marine Expeditionary Force Mar 05
  2d Marine Division Mar 05
  2d Brigade, 2d Infantry Division Aug 04-Aug 05
  155th Armored Brigade Feb 05
  2d Brigade, 26th Infantry Division (M) Aug 05

Cross Boundary Operations
MND-B Apr-Jul 04
Fights Mahdi Army in MND-CS sector
I MEF Aug 04
(With elements of 1st Cavalry Division)
Fights Mahdi Army in Najaf in MND-CS sector and
"Triangle of Death"
MND-B 2004-05
Operates in "Triangle of Death" area south of Baghdad in
Babil Province

Multinational Division-Baghdad (MND-B)
1st Armored Division May 03-Apr 04
  2d Cavalry Regiment (Light) May 03-May 04
  2d Brigade, 82d Airborne Division Apr 03-Apr 04
1st Cavalry Division Apr 04-Feb 05
  2d Brigade, 10th Mountain Division (Light Inf) Mar 04-Mar 05
  39th Infantry Brigade Mar 04-Mar 05
  256th Infantry Brigade (Mechanized) Oct 04-Oct 05
  2d Brigade, 82d Airborne Division Dec 04-Apr 05
3d Infantry Division (Mechanized) Feb 05
  3d Brigade, 1st Armored Division Feb 05
  48th Infantry Brigade (Mechanized) Jun 05

Multinational Division-Central South (MND-CS)
12th (PO) Mechanized Division Sep 03-Jan 04
16th (PO) Pomeranian Mechanized Division Jan 04-Jul 04
1st (PO) Warsaw Mechanized Division Jul 04-Jan 05
11th (PO) Lubusz Armored Cavalry Division Jan 05-Jul 05

Multinational Division-Southeast (MND-SE)
3d Armoured Div (UK) Jul 03-Apr 04
(composite UK Div Staff since Apr 04)

Figure 28. Unit rotations in Iraq, 2003-2005.

than 140,000 in response to the increasing intensity of the insurgency.[8] Additionally, the March 2004 terrorist attack in Madrid, Spain, and the election of a new government there resulted in the withdrawal of a brigade-size contingent of Spanish peacekeepers. This withdrawal, however, did not permanently affect the number of soldiers available because South Korea deployed a force equivalent to a large brigade to northeastern Iraq several months later.[9] See figure 28 for occupation troop rotations in Iraq from July 2003 through January 2005.

Combat operations during the occupation were focused primarily on the Sunni-Arab insurgency near Baghdad and Fallujah and in the north near Mosul, and on the Shiite uprising led by Muqtada al-Sadr and his Mahdi Army militia in Baghdad and Najaf. Military forces were also responsible for securing the January 2005 general elections and the October 2005 constitutional referendum. The intensity of combat, represented by US combat-related deaths, peaked during the periods of combat operations against major insurgent forces.[10] See figure 29.

In April 2004 US forces faced the twin threat of Sunni resistance in the Anbar Province city of Fallujah, 50 miles west of Baghdad, and Shiite intransigence in the Sadr City section of Baghdad and in the Shiite holy city of Najaf. Actions against both groups ended without resolution. Marine forces ended their siege of Fallujah at the end of the month, and Sadr signed a truce agreement on 4 June.

The truce was short-lived and in August 2004 forces from I MEF and the Iraqi security forces massed against Sadr's Mahdi Army militia in Najaf. They quickly compressed Sadr's forces into the precincts near the Shiite Imam Ali shrine. This resulted in a standoff that did not favor Sadr. After the intervention of other Shiite factions, Sadr again agreed to a cease-fire in Najaf and later in Sadr City, after which he agreed to participate in the January 2005 electoral process.

Fallujah, meanwhile, had become a bastion for the Sunni insurgent forces primarily led by the Jordanian, Abu Musab al-Zarqawi. A combined Marine-Army force cordoned off Fallujah in November 2004 and systematically assaulted and cleared the city over the course of eight days.

In addition to these major operations, the insurgents, using terror tactics almost on a daily basis, opposed the occupation and the development of new Iraqi civil and military structures. These terror tactics consisted of the employment of scores of fanatical suicide bombers, convoy ambushes, snipers equipped with light rocket propelled grenade launchers (RPG), and a variety of improvised explosive devices (IED) placed along

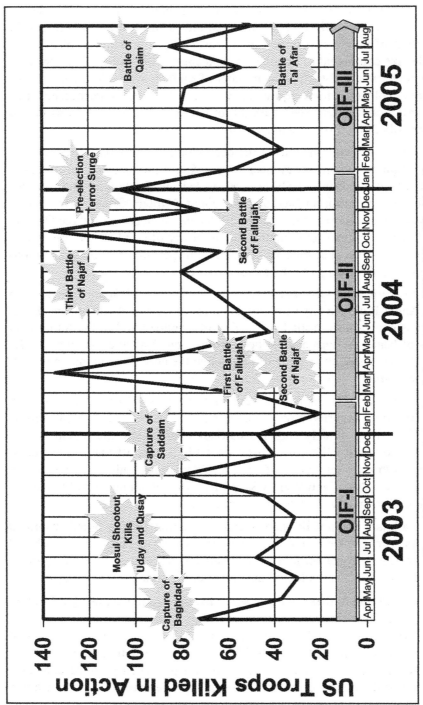

Figure 29. Intensity of operations in Iraq in terms of US soldiers killed in action.

roads or in vehicles and remote detonated. The homicidal suicide bombers consisted primarily of non-Iraqi, Islamic fanatics, serving loosely under the banner of Zarqawi, the operative who had also masterminded the resistance in Fallujah.[11]

In late June 2004, the new Iraqi provisional government led by interim Prime Minister Iyad Allawi assumed sovereignty for Iraq from the CPA. Allawi was a prominent Shiite who had lived in exile in Britain and had been a member of the Iraqi Governing Council (IGC). Bremer had established the IGC in July 2003 initially to draft a new Iraqi constitution. Failing at this, the IGC, in coordination with the American authorities, prepared a plan to transition Iraq to a new sovereign, civilian government. Initially, the new scheme called for the establishment of an interim government in June 2004 to govern Iraq until the national elections on 31 January 2005 would elect a transitional government to draft a national constitution. After these elections, a national referendum to approve the proposed constitution would be held in October 2005. If voters approved the constitution, which they did by a narrow margin, provisions of the new constitution would be implemented to establish a permanent government.

Allawi led the interim government from June 2004 to January 2005. After the January 2005 elections, Prime Minister Ibrahim al-Jafari, another former Shiite exile, and President Jalal Talabani, the most prominent Kurdish politician, led the new Iraqi transitional government.

As the end of OIF-II approached in early 2005, so too did the first Iraqi general elections. Because of the added security concerns and the increased intensity of insurgent attacks in the weeks and months leading up to the elections, troop density did not drop drastically during the transition from OIF-II to OIF-III as it had between OIF-I and OIF-II. In fact, US force strength increased before the elections, reaching about 160,000 in January 2005.[12] This represented an augmentation of about 20,000 from the 2004 average numbers and occurred due to a combination of the early arrival of several OIF-III brigades and the temporary deployment of troops from the 2d Brigade, 82d Airborne Division, to augment forces in Baghdad. The overlapping of OIF-II and OIF-III forces not only allowed the rotation to be staggered, but also temporarily increased the number of forces available during the elections.[13]

This was only transitory. After the handoff to the OIF-III rotation, completed by May 2005, troop force levels fell back to 140,000. During OIF-III the XVIII Airborne Corps replaced the III Corps as the MNC-I. OIF-III also included the first use of a reserve component, division headquarters, the 42d Infantry Division (Mechanized), New York Army National Guard, as the MND-NC. In addition to the 42d, during OIF-III, five Army National

Guard brigades were deployed throughout the occupation force. OIF-III was also the first time units organized under the Army's new modularity concept deployed. The 3d Infantry Division (Mechanized) returned to Baghdad configured under the new structure. OIF-III also marked the return of a larger force to the Mosul area, as an armored cavalry regiment headquarters, an armored cavalry regiment, and a Stryker brigade replaced the brigade-size Task Force Olympia.

Due to growing security concerns as the October 2005 Iraqi constitutional referendum vote approached, US forces were increased by about 12,000 troops. This plus up was completed by overlapping OIF-III and early OIF-IV unit deployments and through the dispatch of several smaller units to reinforce the theater forces.[14]

As early as December 2004, the US Department of Defense had begun programming for the 2005-06 OIF-IV rotation. To accommodate the projected December 2005 Iraqi general elections, redeployment dates for about 10,000 troops were extended into 2006.[15] Even before the October 2005 referendum, however, there were clear indications the year 2006 could mark a reduction in US troops as trained Iraqi security forces assumed security responsibilities.[16]

Geographical Area, Terrain, and Population Density

The area of Iraq is 167,617 square miles. In 2003 US Army planners estimated the population at 25.5 million. Nationwide, Iraq has a population density of 152.13 people per square mile. However, this figure is deceptive as whole tracts of Iraq are uninhabited desert, while other areas, primarily in the fertile valleys of the Tigris and Euphrates rivers, are much more densely settled. Up to 68 percent of the population lives in urban areas. The population of the Baghdad metropolitan area is 6.2 million people packed into 283 square miles, giving Baghdad a population density of 21,908.1 people per square mile, comparable to New York City's population density of 25,025 people per square mile.[17]

The population of Iraq is not homogeneous, but consists primarily of two distinct ethnic groups, Arabs and Kurds. The Kurds, about 18 percent of the population or 4 million strong, speak an Iranian language related distantly to Persian and live primarily in the north and northeast areas of Iraq. Kurds also live in neighboring parts of Iran and Turkey. In the 1990s, the Iraqi Kurds had maintained an autonomous status in Iraq after many conflicts with the central government in Baghdad. The Kurds are Islamic, primarily of the Sunni sect. In addition to the Kurds, small numbers of Turkmen (speaking a language related to Turkish) live in northern Iraq.[18]

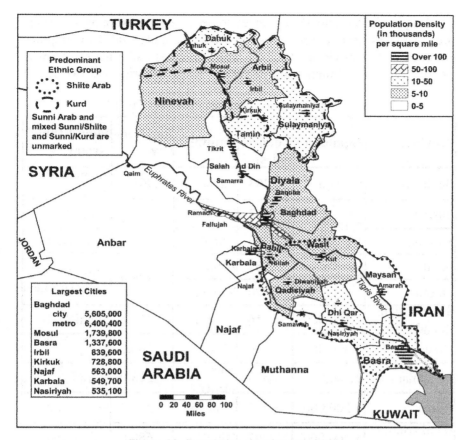

Figure 30. Population density, Iraq 2003.

Arabs are the other major ethnic group in Iraq. While all Arabs speak the Iraqi dialect of Arabic, religion divides the Arabs into two subgroups: the majority Shiites (60 percent) and the minority Sunnis (35 percent), and a small group of Christians (5 percent) who are somewhat anachronistically referred to as Assyrians or Chaldeans. Some or all of the Christian groups, while all speak Arabic, also speak another Semitic language called Aramaic or Syriac. The Shiites live primarily in Baghdad and in the southern portion of the country near the two main shrines of the Shiite sect at Najaf and Karbala. The Sunni Arabs are concentrated in the central portion of the country around Baghdad and along the Tigris and Euphrates rivers to the north and east. There had also been deliberate Sunni settlement in the southern portions of the Kurdish area under the Baathist regime, particularly around the city of Mosul. Figure 30 depicts population density and ethnic group dispersion in Iraq.

Iraq is divided into 18 provinces sometimes referred to as governor-ates. Table 14 lists the provinces, provincial capitals, and demographics for each of the provinces. In 2003 nine provinces had a majority Shiite population, two a Sunni majority, two a Kurd majority and two had a

Table 14. Demographics in Iraq Provinces, 2003[19]

Province	Population	Area (square miles)	Capital	Pop Density	Main Ethnic Group
Baghdad	6,200,000	283	Baghdad	21,908.1	Sunni & Shiite Arab
Basrah	2,400,000	7363	Basra	325.9	Shiite Arab
Maysan		6205	Amarah		Shiite Arab
Arbil	2,100,000	5587	Arbil	375.9	Kurd/ Sunni Arab/Turkmen
Ta'mim		3970	Kirkuk		
Salah ad-Din (Saladin)	1,100,000	9556	Samarra	115.1	Sunni Arab
Nineva	2,400,000	14,410	Mosul	166.5	Sunni Arab/ Kurd
Sulaymaniyah	1,400,000	6573	Sulaymaniyah	213.0	Kurd
Anbar	1,200,000	53,476	Ramadi	224.4	Sunni Arab
Babil (Babylonia)	1,700,000	2497	Hillah	680.8	Shiite Arab
Najaf	900,000	11,129	Najaf	80.9	Shiite Arab
Karbala	700,000	1944	Karbala	360.1	Shiite Arab
Dhi Qar	1,400,000	4981	Nasiriyah	281.1	Shiite Arab
Wasit	860,000	6623	Kut	129.9	Shiite Arab
Diyala	961,073	7365	Ba'quba	190.1	Sunni & Shiite Arab
Dahuk	450,000	2530	Dahuk	177.9	Kurd
Qadisiyah	850,000	3148	Diwaniyah	270.0	Shiite Arab
Muthanna	480,000	19,977	Samawah	24.0	Shiite Arab
18 provinces	25,500,000	167,617			

mixed Sunni-Shiite population, while the remaining three had a mixed Sunni-Kurd population.[20]

An analysis of the 2003 population densities of the 18 provinces (with several grouped together as American planners did prior to the start of US operations there) shows two provinces (Baghdad, Babil) had a population density more than three times the national average, while three others were more than double the national average (Basrah-Maysan, Arbil-Ta'mim, and Karbala). At the other extreme, the provinces of Muthanna, consisting mostly of desert bordering on Saudi Arabia, and Najaf, which, except for the city of Najaf, is empty desert, were two times less dense than the national average.

Troop Deployment and Organization

Planning for the occupation of Iraq was concurrent with the planning for the Baghdad campaign. The chief of the CFLCC C5 (Plans) section, Colonel Kevin Benson, has outlined how his staff section estimated the minimum projected force density needed for the occupation phase of Operation IRAQI FREEDOM.[21] Initially, the planners looked at the area and population of Iraq, emphasizing demographic factors, but ensuring force coverage for the whole country. Then Benson's team determined the number of combat troops needed to perform occupation activities. Planners used a brigade of four battalions as the basic building block, and the Iraqi province as the basic deployment area, emphasizing coverage in all of the major cities. Planners prioritized the cities and provinces beginning with Baghdad. For a rough estimate of the number of brigades needed, Benson looked at the example of local police forces in the state of California as a guideline.[22]

Benson's planning presumed an unknown level of indigenous support from the former Iraqi police and military forces.[23] The projected minimum force levels included all Coalition land forces, Marines, and multinational elements. Table 15 and figure 31 illustrate the results of the CFLCC C5 planning.

This planning estimate resulted in a minimum force of 20 brigade equivalents, interpolated as a force of 125,000 combat troops and 175,000 non-combat support and command and control troops for a total force of 300,000.[24] The C5 estimate would soon prove to be too optimistic, both in number of brigades and in the placement of forces. While the estimate provided for a force of 20 brigades for the whole Coalition, throughout the occupation, American forces alone averaged between 17 and 20 brigade equivalents, the multinational forces supplied an additional 5.25 brigades,

Table 15. Planning Factors for Iraq Occupation Force

Priority	Planned No of Bdes	Province	Population	Area (square mile)	Pop Density
1	6	Baghdad	6,200,000	283	21,908.1
2	2	Basrah	2,400,000	7363	325.9
		Maysan		6205	
3	3	Arbil	2,100,000	5587	375.9
		Ta'mim		3970	
4	2	Salah ad-Din	1,100,000	9556	115.1
5	1	Nineva	2,400,000	14,410	166.5
6	1	Sulaymaniyah	1,400,000	6573	213.0
7	1	Anbar	1,200,000	53,476	224.4
8	0.5	Babil	1,700,000	2497	680.8
9	0.75	Najaf	900,000	11,129	80.9
10	0.5	Karbala	700,000	1944	360.1
11	1	Dhi Qar	1,400,000	4981	281.1
12	0.5	Wasit	860,000	6623	129.9
13	0.25	Diyala	961,073	7365	190.1
14	0.25	Dahuk	450,000	2530	177.9
15	0.25	Qadisiyah	850,000	3148	270.0
16	0	Muthanna	480,000	19,977	24.0
Totals	20	18 provinces	25,500,000	167,617	

equating to a peak total force of 25.25 brigade equivalents in January 2005.[25] At this time, there were 184,500 troops in Iraq, 160,000 of which were American.[26] Overall, each brigade equivalent and support slice averaged 7306.93 troops, 8000 per American brigade and 4666.66 per Coalition brigade. In January 2005 at the peak of US force size there were five more brigades deployed than the planners had estimated. However, the actual size of the brigade equivalents and related support slice was roughly half of what they had projected, 7306.93 versus 15,000 personnel per brigade and the total force strength was just over half the number of troops planners estimated would be needed, 184,500 versus 300,000. See figure 32 for a graph of US force strength in Iraq from 2003-05.

Apart from force size, brigade areas of responsibility were, for the most part, consistent with projections. The one anomaly was Anbar Province. Although mostly uninhabited desert, two key Sunni cities were located in eastern Anbar Province, Ramadi and Fallujah, and in northern Anbar, several large Sunni settlements existed along the Euphrates River

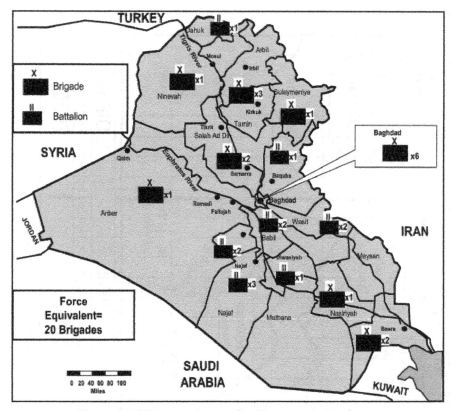

Figure 31. Minimum planned Coalition occupation force.

extending from the Baghdad area to Syria. Benson's planners believed one brigade could cover this area. In the early days of the occupation, the 3d ACR was the sole Coalition force for the province. However, it quickly became apparent the armored cavalry troopers would have to be augmented by the 3d Infantry Division (Mechanized), which was shifted from Baghdad to Anbar. From this point forward, an equivalent of four brigades would garrison Anbar.

Troop organization has been discussed in the situational narrative. As in Bosnia and Kosovo, Coalition forces established placeholder multinational commands in Iraq, which remained in place while headquarters and units rotated in and out to assume their mission. In an unusual move, large artillery units from the 1st Cavalry Division, 1st Armored Division, and 197th Field Artillery Brigade deployed, not as firing units, but as motorized patrol and security units. While the other nations in the Coalition created special units for the occupation, American forces were composed of preexisting units, although at the brigade and division level, units were

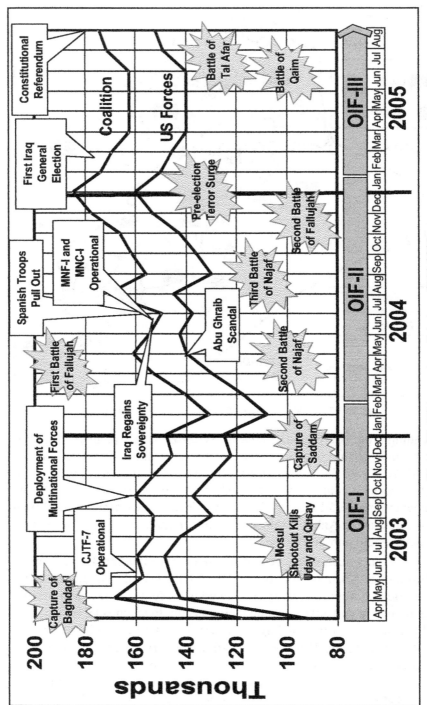

Figure 32. US troop strength in Iraq, 2003-2005.

often mixed and matched, with reserve component battalions and brigades attached to augment or replace organic active units. In early 2005 the first four-brigade modular division force, the 3d Infantry Division (Mechanized), was dispatched to Baghdad. For the mission in Iraq, the division's four brigades were separated. Two of the brigades were attached to the 42d Infantry Division and the remaining two served under the parent division, which was then augmented by a brigade from the 1st Armored Division and an Army National Guard brigade. See figure 33 for actual brigade deployment locations.

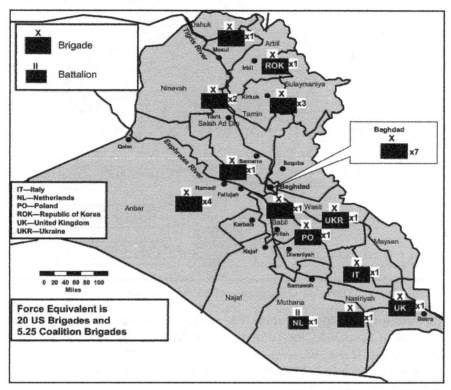

Figure 33. Actual brigade deployment for the occupation of Iraq.

The city of Baghdad is a good example of how the occupation/contingency operation was managed in terms of organization and troop density in an urban environment. For the 2003 Baghdad campaign and the contingency operation, operational planners divided Baghdad into 55 tactical zones or sectors, each numbered in order of relative importance.

As in the rest of the country (where the province boundaries marked areas of responsibility), the zones in Baghdad delineated the areas of

127

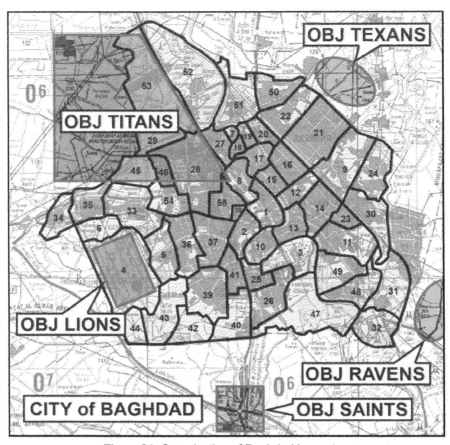

Figure 34. Organization of Baghdad by sector.

responsibility for specific units. For example, during its brief time in Baghdad in April 2003, the 101st Airborne Division (Air Assault) was responsible for clearing the ten sectors of southwestern Baghdad, west of the Tigris River (sectors 3, 25-6, 39-44 and 47).[27] See figure 34 for the sector organization of Baghdad.

Indigenous Support

Initially, the occupation force in Iraq, after concluding a victorious campaign against the Baathist regime, could not and did not count on any indigenous support. On 23 May 2003 Bremer issued CPA Order Number 2 officially dissolving the Iraqi armed forces and associated security forces, which together had numbered about 400,000 prior to the Baghdad campaign. While these forces no longer existed as organized units after most had dissolved of their own accord rather than being destroyed in battle, there had been speculation some of the less politicized elements of the former Baathist regime's armed forces could be used as a basis for a new Iraqi army.[28]

Under orders issued on 7 August 2003, Bremer created new Iraqi armed forces. The new forces were originally a complicated grouping of various defense agencies: a civil defense corps designed for local self-defense, an intervention force specially trained in urban counterinsurgency tactics, and various other small agencies, as well as a three-division, regular army designed to fight foreign threats. All of these forces eventually fell under the Ministry of Defense of the several transitory Iraqi governments. By far, the civil defense corps was the largest of these forces in terms of recruited personnel. In January 2004 this corps was given a more national-level mission and redesignated as the Iraqi National Guard. A year later, its forces were amalgamated into the army, as were various other small military forces such as the Iraqi Intervention Force. At the same time, the Iraqi Ministry of the Interior was fielding various police forces, including a general police force, the Iraqi Police Service, a mechanized reaction force (eventually the size of a division), a border patrol, and several smaller agencies. [29]

The total size of the joint Ministry of Defense and Ministry of the Interior's Iraqi Security Forces (ISF) from October 2003 to October 2005 is shown in figure 35. The Iraqis never suffered from a lack of volunteers for all their services, despite cyclic insurgent attacks directed at the ISF. After the January 2005 elections, even Sunni Arabs began volunteering for the forces in proportional numbers.[30] However, the ISF suffered from a slow start in 2003-04 because of frequent changes in its force structure and mission, partially due to the fact three different governments ruled Iraq between late 2004 and early 2005, and partially due to a variety of other miscalculations. Therefore, it was not until mid-2004 when the ISF began training in significant numbers and receiving adequate equipment to participate effectively in combat operations.[31]

Actual, effective strength of the ISF often differed from the reported strength. For example, when the Iraqi government reviewed the police force numbers in detail in mid-2004, they found up to 100,000 of the officers reported proved to be unfit, nonexistent, or deserters. After such scrutiny, the police force size dropped by two-thirds in the last half of 2004, but this revised strength was a more accurate picture of the qualified police force.[32]

The long-term objective was for ISF elements to relieve Coalition troops from their occupation duties. However, when Coalition troop

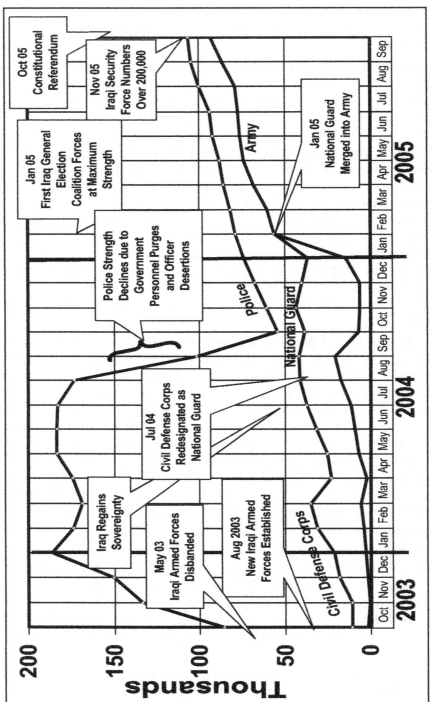

Figure 35. Iraqi security forces strength during US occupation, 2003-2005.

deployments reached their zenith in January 2005, ISF had yet to take over any operational missions. It was not until late February when the first Iraqi army brigade assumed an area of operations in Baghdad from an American unit.[33]

Throughout 2005, Iraqi army units assumed an increasing number of roles and missions and took over more camps and forward operating bases from Coalition troops. The ISF took on a more sectarian appearance as, by mid-2005, three Kurds, three Shiite Arabs, three Sunni Arabs, and a Turk-men commanded the 10 Iraqi army divisions.[34] **See figure 36 for locations** of active Iraqi Security Forces in June and September 2005.

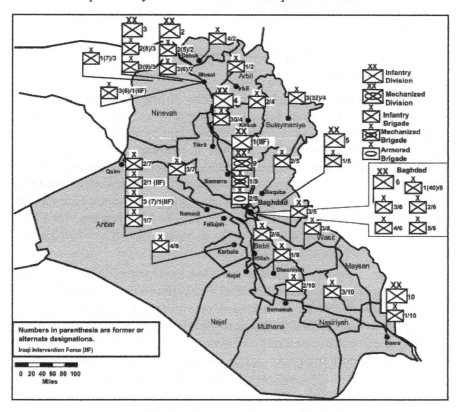

Figure 36. Location of Iraqi army units, 2005.

Although some questioned the overall readiness and capability of the Iraqi forces, they provided the bulk of the security for the October 2005 **referendum and were projected to do so for the December 2005 general** elections. Iraq president Jalal Talabani expected the ISF to be able take over for 50,000 Coalition troops by the end of 2005, although the US

OIF-IV troop rotation had already commenced in November 2005 without any reduction in troops.[35]

By all objective standards, however, the ISF had shown remarkable progress since July 2004 when it had no operational battalions at the national level. In the later part of 2005, the Iraqi army began expanding its own logistic support capabilities.[36] By December 2005 projections were for an operational force at the national level of 106 battalions, organized into 35 brigades and 10 divisions, and an additional 10 specialized police battalions. By June 2006 the number of battalions was expected to increase to 114. In October 2005 ISF strength crossed the 200,000 threshold, with a projected strength of 230,000 by December 2005 and 270,000 by June 2006.[37]

Iraq Operation Analysis

The Force Size Debate

The size of the force for the occupation of Iraq has been a hotly debated issue. One of the main focal points of this debate has been comments made by General Eric Shinseki, then Army Chief of Staff, while testifying to the Senate Armed Services Committee in February 2003. When asked, General Shinseki commented he felt the occupation would require several hundred thousand soldiers, an estimate interpreted in this work as 300,000. Shinseki had a background in the Balkan occupations as the commander of the SFOR in 1997 and 1998. Following that, he had been the Vice Chief of Staff, then Chief of Staff of the Army during the 1999 Kosovo crisis and subsequent deployment.

Newspaper reports claimed at the time Pentagon officials disagreed with Shinseki's proposed 300,000 total and believed the figure to be closer to 100,000. However, as discussed previously, Benson, as the chief Army planner for the occupation force, projected at a minimum a force of 125,000 combat troops alone. He also estimated an additional 125,000 to 175,000 support troops, bringing the total force projection closer to Shinseki's 300,000 total. As stated, the combat force actually deployed was larger than Benson's estimate, but the tooth-to-tail ratio was a good bit smaller.[38]

The commanders in the field have never said there was a troop shortage in Iraq and believed when they requested an increase in forces, for example, during the Fallujah and Najaf crises in 2004, they were provided all the troops they asked for. General John Abizaid, the US Central Command (CENTCOM) commander, not only reiterated this, but also stated what he believed was needed in Iraq was a greater role for Iraqi security forces and Coalition troops from Islamic countries, rather than additional US forces.[39]

In many ways, the force size debate has come full circle as some commanders and military observers are ultimately arguing for a smaller force or claiming only the new Iraqi armed forces can defeat the insurgency, though those same observers often cite the purported low quality of those forces.[40]

Troop Density in Iraq

Table 16 provides a summary of troop density in the Iraq contingency operation. Coalition forces deployed a maximum of 1.10 soldiers per square mile nationwide. However, this included large swathes of

Table 16. Troop Density in Iraq, 2003-2005

Area	Military Forces (at maximum)	Population	Area (square miles)	Population Density (per square mile)	Soldier Density		
					Per Area (soldiers per square mile)	Per Population (1 soldier per x residents)	Soldiers Per 1000 People
Iraq							
Planned	300,000				1.79	85.0	11.76
Planned (smaller tooth-to-tail ratio)	146,139	25.5 million	167,617	152.13	0.87	174.5	5.73
Actual	184,500				1.10	138.2	7.23
Baghdad							
Planned	89,985				317.57	68.9	14.52
Planned (smaller tooth-to-tail ratio)	48,000	6.2 million	283.4	21,878.61	169.37	129.2	7.74
Actual	56,000				197.6	110.7	9.03

uninhabited territory. The ratio was much higher in the urban area of Baghdad: 176 troops per square mile. In terms of demographics, the Coalition at its maximum deployed 1 soldier for every 139 inhabitants, or 7.26 soldiers per 1000 local inhabitants. In Baghdad, again the ratios were much higher, with 1 soldier for every 177 Baghdad residents or 9.03 soldiers per 1000 city residents. Table 16 also displays Benson's planning figures and a modified version of them using the smaller tooth-to-tail ratio actually employed by the deployed force. Benson's original figures were all considerably higher than those of the force actually deployed (although his planning force of 17 to 20 brigades was actually about five brigades less than the number actually deployed). His planning estimates modified to include the actual tooth-to-tail ratio were, however, all smaller than the forces actually deployed.

Indigenous forces, although increasing in size and effectiveness over the course of time, were not really a factor in troop density determinations in the Iraq occupation, as no Iraqi forces relieved Coalition forces of any occupation responsibilities until after the maximum force was deployed in January 2005. Iraqi security forces augmented but did not replace Coalition forces until February 2005.

Analysis of the Factors Affecting Troop Density

The previous chapter analyzed the various factors affecting troop density in contingency operations using the operations studied earlier in this work. The same factors will now be similarly analyzed in terms of the Iraq operation.

Iraq has both a large population and a large area. However, large portions of the population are concentrated in urban and suburban areas, particularly in Baghdad where the population density approaches that of New York. Therefore, Baghdad is a relatively compact area of responsibility with a high population density

The number of troops available initially for the Iraq contingency operation was actually less than those available shortly thereafter and in subsequent months when additional reinforcements arrived in the theater. Because the previous campaign emphasized defeating the Iraqi forces, not occupation locations, troops deployed more densely in certain areas than in others. For example, because the city of Baghdad was the objective of the campaign, most of the large units ultimately converged there. In fact, in the early days of the contingency operation, the equivalent of three divisions (roughly between 10 and 13 brigade equivalents) was operating in the Baghdad area. For most of the extended operation, however,

Baghdad was the responsibility of a single reinforced division (seven brigade equivalents).

Additionally, the troops deployed for contingency operations in Iraq were not recruited specifically for the operation. US troops deployed in preexisting units, on a 12-month troop rotation cycle for the Army and seven months for the Marines. Coalition troops generally rotated every six months.

In relation to the duration and intensity factor studied in other operations, Iraq has proven to be a counterinsurgency operation of extended duration and a continuous high level of intensity. Accordingly, deployed forces reached the height of their strength not at the beginning of the operation, but in January 2005.

Another key factor in this study is the use of substitute forces in contingency operations. In Iraq substitute forces have been primarily civilian contractors. Confirmed numbers of contractors supporting the Iraq operation are inconsistent. Estimates range between 20,000 and 100,000 cited from various sources and contexts. It is, however, clear there are about 20,000 employees of private military corporations (PMC) devoted solely to security functions. In previous operations soldiers or local police officers would have been responsible for these security functions. In addition to security contractors, other civilian contractors provide necessary support services, such as transportation, construction, and food service, functions that have also historically been the responsibility of military forces.

Contractor Kellogg, Brown and Root (KBR) at one point employed approximately 24,000 workers to conduct support functions, increasing the number of nonsecurity contractors to somewhere in the range of 30,000 to 80,000. For the purpose of this study, a mean of 58,000 contractors is added to the security contractor estimate of 20,000 for a total estimated contractor strength in Iraq of 78,000. This interpolated figure is considered the estimated number of contractors in Iraq at the height of Coalition deployment in January 2005. Because of the important role contractors play in Iraq, they are a key factor in any discussion of troop density.[42]

As noted, the key factors in studying troop density in Iraq are indigenous forces and substitute forces. At the maximum deployment of ground troops in Iraq in January 2005, indigenous forces had not yet taken over any operational missions, so there can be no adjustment to the troop figures to include indigenous forces. However, substitute forces in the form of contractor personnel, with an estimated total of 78,000, played a key role. Augmenting the 184,500 Coalition troops in Iraq with 78,000

Table 17. Iraq and Troop Density Variation in Terms of Key Factors

		Troop Density (+/- adjusted mean of 13.26 soldiers per 1000 population)	Dense Area	Troops Available	Troop Rotation	Troops Recruited	Intensity/ Duration	Substitute Forces	Indigenous forces
Malaya		11.44		•	•	•	•	•	•
Kosovo		7.84	•		•				
Germany 1 year	More ↑	2.44		•					
Bosnia IFOR		1.74	•	•	•				
Austria		0.11		•					•
Northern Luzon	Troops	-0.76			•	•	•		
Iraq		-2.97			•	•	•		
Philippines		-3.46			•	•	•		
Bosnia SFOR	Fewer ↓	-5.36	•	•	•				•
Germany 2 years		-6.88							•
Japan		-7.06		•					•

contractors adjusts the strength to 262,500. This represents a troop density of 97.14 inhabitants per soldier, 5.32 inhabitants per soldier less dense than the planning figure of 91.82. In terms of troops per 1000 inhabitants, this corresponds to a ratio of 10.29 troops per 1000 residents, 2.97 soldiers per 1000 less than the recommended planning ratio of 13.26 per 1000 residents.

Table 17 represents how the Iraq deployment fits proportionally with the historical trends in troop density examined in this work. While not the densest deployment, the Iraq operation is in the middle range among the analyzed case studies. Overall, how does the Iraq operation relate to historical trends in troop density? Table 18 shows the results of a comparison between the troop density figures for the Iraq operation with the planning factors derived from the case studies examined in this work.

Table 18. Applying the Planning Factors to the Iraq Deployment

(a)	**Planning Factors**	
(a1)	Population of Iraq	25.5 million
(a2)	Adjusted raw force planning factor	13.26 soldiers per 1000 of population
		91.82 inhabitants per soldier
(a3)	Brigade equivalent planning factor size	5909 troops
(a4)	Brigade equivalent to population ratio	One brigade per 483,141 inhabitants
(b)	**Expected Deployment Size**	
(b1)	Expected adjusted force size estimate (a1/a2)	277,748
(b2)	Number of brigades expected (b1/a3)	47
(c)	**Actual Deployment**	
(c1)	Maximum force size	184,500 (January 2005)
(c2)	Maximum adjusted force size	262,500 (January 2005) (184,500 Troops +78,000 Contractors).
(c3)	Adjusted troop density ratio c2/(a1/1000) (a1/c2)	10.29 soldiers per 1000 of population
		97.14 inhabitants per soldier
(c4)	Number of brigades actually deployed	25.25 (January 2005)
(c5)	Actual brigade size (c1/c4)	7307
(c6)	Adjusted number of brigade equivalents ([c2-c1]/c5)+c4	35.9
(c7)	Brigade equivalent to population ratio (a1/c6)	One brigade per 709,816 inhabitants.
(d)	**Differences**	
(d1)	Adjusted force size difference (b1-c2)	-15,217 troops deployed
(d2)	Difference from force planning factor (a2-c3)	-2.97 soldiers per 1000 of population
		+5.32 inhabitants per soldier
(d3)	Number of brigade equivalents difference (b2-c6)	-11.1 brigade-equivalents
(d4)	Adjusted brigade size (a3-c5)	+1,398 troops per brigade equivalent
(d5)	Brigade equivalent to population ratio difference (c6-a4)	+226,625 inhabitants per one brigade equivalent

The OIF actual deployment numbers were 15,217 below the planning figure estimate, 95 percent of the projected total or roughly the size of two brigade equivalents. Additionally, the actual deployment figures were slightly less dense than the planning factor ratio by approximately 3 troops per 1000 of population. In terms of expected operational units, the total force brigade-equivalent, however, was roughly 11 brigade equivalents (or 24 percent) below the estimated planning factor. However, brigade equivalents for the Iraq deployment were 124 percent larger than the projected size of a brigade equivalent during the planning process, meaning the 35.9 adjusted brigade equivalents (see table 18) were in fact equivalent in size to 44.5 planning factor brigade equivalents. This corresponds to the force-size difference of 15,217, which, as stated above, is roughly equivalent to two Iraq deployment brigade equivalents.

In terms of the Iraq operation, the maximum troop deployment period was in January 2005. At that time, the 124,733 Iraqi forces had not yet taken an operational role. Therefore, these troops and police forces were not taken into account. Additionally, the estimated 78,000 contractors in Iraq were not all executing operational missions, but they are included in total force estimates because their presence in Iraq, even in supporting roles, effectively released military personnel for roles more directly related to combat operations.

Therefore, in January 2005, the number of troops deployed in Iraq, including operational contractor elements, was slightly less than projected by the planning factors in raw troop strength and in proportion to the population. Total force operational brigades in Iraq, while about 11 brigades below the expected planning factor level, were proportionally larger than the planning factor brigade size, which accounts for the variance ultimately resulting in a force slightly more than two brigades smaller than the planning factor estimate.

Notes

1.   Michael Hersh and John Barry, "Drawing down in Iraq: Drastic Troop Cuts are in the Pentagon's Secret Plans," *Newsweek*, 8 August 2005 [article on-line] available at http://www.msnbc.msn.com/id/8770418/site/newsweek/; Internet; accessed 24 October 2005; Jim VandeHei, "Talabani Says Iraqis Could Replace Many U.S. Troops: President's Claim About Major American Withdrawal by Year's End Conflicts With White House Position," *Washington Post*, 13 September 2005, A20 [article on-line] available at http://www.washingtonpost.com/wp-dyn/content/article/2005/09/12/AR2005091201986.html; Internet; accessed 24 October 2005.

2.   Before the arrival of multinational Coalition forces, US forces reached a height of 148,750 in July 2003. Force size fluctuations in early 2004 were primarily based on unit rotation overlaps. The primary US forces withdrawn without rotational American replacement were the roughly 25,000 Marines of the I Marine Expeditionary Force, which handed its sector of responsibility over to a Polish division and to an Italian brigade serving under the British, whose own sector was accordingly extended. British forces originally numbered about 26,000, but were reduced from three to one brigade, with replacements including a Dutch battalion and the aforementioned Italian brigade. For a table of US ground forces numbers, see "US Ground Troops in Iraq," 27 April 2005 [website on-line] available at http://www.globalsecurity.org/military/ops/iraq_orbat_es.htm; Internet; accessed 24 October 2005.

3.   The sector in Anbar Province would be later given over to the Marines who commanded it with a MEF headquarters (although usually only employing a division-equivalent of land forces), giving the Marine commander in Anbar the same rank (lieutenant general) as the Army commander of CJTF-7 in Baghdad, the higher command echelon for the MEF.

4.   The Polish forces were mandated by their government to only engage in security operations. See Associated Press, "Polish Commander Urges Early Iraq Vote," 30 August 2004, [document on-line] available at http://www.wjla.com/news/stories/0804/169623.html; Internet; accessed 25 October 2005.

5.   A rationale for the shorter rotation periods of non-American forces can be found in Andrew A. Michta, "Military Capabilities of the Central Europeans: What Can They Contribute to the Stabilization of Iraq?" (summary of lecture from the Eastern European Studies at the Woodrow Wilson International Center for Scholars, Washington, DC, 2003, meeting #284) [meeting report on-line] available at http://www.wilsoncenter.org/index.cfm?fuseaction=topics.print_pub&doc_id=54116&group_id=7427&topic_id=1422&stoplayout=true; Internet; accessed 24 October 2005. Active duty US army units were on a 12/12 plan, deploying for 12 months and then exempt from deployment for the next 12 months. US Marine Corps units, except higher headquarters, were on a 7/7 plan, seven-month deployments followed by a seven-month break from deployment eligibility. See "Troop Move Will Not Reduce Korean Security, Officials Say," (press briefing by senior defense and military officials, 17 May 2004) 18 May 2004 [transcripts on-line]

available at http://usinfo.state.gov/xarchives/display.html?p=washfile-english& y=2004&m=May&x=20040518135243AJesroM8.613223e-02&t=xarchives/xar chitem.html; Internet; accessed 28 October 2005.

6. The 82d Airborne Division had replaced the 3d Infantry Division (Mechanized) in Anbar Province in September 2003 as the first rotation. This relief is sometimes considered to be part of OIF II, but the 82d was slated to remain in Anbar for only six months and then redeploy without replacement. The 82d was relieved in March 2004, but the division was in fact replaced in a modification to the OIF II rotation scheme by the Marines of I MEF. See press briefing by General John Keane, acting Army chief of staff, "Gen. Keane Press Briefing on Plans to Rotate Forces in Iraq," (Pentagon press briefing by acting Army chief of staff and other military officials, Washington, DC, 23 July 2003) July 2003 [transcripts online] available at http://www.globalsecurity.org/military/library/news/2003/07/ mil-030723-dod03.htm; Internet; accessed 27 October 2005.

7. The replacement force was officially known as Task Force (TF) Olympia, but its main component was the 3d Brigade, 2d Infantry Division, the Army's first experimental Stryker unit out of Fort Lewis, Washington. This brigade was originally slated to be the replacement for the 3d Armored Cavalry Regiment in Anbar Province, but was shifted to Mosul to replace the proposed multinational division. Almost all the US divisional forces also had task force designations, with most designations, such as TF Ironhorse for the 4th Infantry Division (Mechanized), later replaced by TF Danger (1st Infantry Division [Mechanized]) and then TF Liberty (42d Infantry Division), changing with the units, making the designation somewhat redundant. Some of these designations, however, such as TF Baghdad, were used by all the units, which rotated through Baghdad in turn. In this work, the actual unit designations are used whenever possible. Originally a multinational division, possibly from India or Pakistan, was supposed to assume responsibility for the Mosul area. However, this support never materialized. See Keane press briefing and Colin Robinson, "The U.S. presence in Iraq: Inching toward internationalized 'peace keeping'?" 28 July 2003 [document on-line] available at http://www.cdi.org/friendlyversion/printversion.cfm?documentID=1534; Internet; accessed 26 October 2005.

8. Keane press briefing; Ann Scott Tyson, "Should US Draw Down Troops in Iraq?" *Christian Science Monitor,* 23 October 2003. [article on-line] available at http://www.csmonitor.com/2003/1023/p02s02-usmi.html; Internet; accessed 26 October 2005. As originally planned, the 82d Airborne Division force in Anbar Province was not to be replaced. The 3d ACR, originally attached to the 82d, was, however, to be replaced by the 3d Brigade, 2d Infantry Division. However that brigade was diverted to Mosul and the 3d ACR was replaced by the 1st Brigade, 1st Infantry Division (Mechanized). The Marine Corps' I MEF replaced the 82d. The 2d Brigade, 82d Airborne Division, detached from its parent division and serving under the 1st Armored Division in Baghdad, was also originally not scheduled for a replacement. However, the 2d Brigade, 10th Mountain Division (Light Infantry) replaced it and served under the 1st Armored Division's successor unit, the 1st Cavalry Division.

9. The Korean force was styled the "Zaytun" Division, using the Arabic term for "olive," a metaphor for peace. Despite its designation as a division, the Republic of Korea (ROK) contingent was only about 3,000 soldiers in size, roughly equivalent to a brigade. The Korean force was given the predominately Kurdish Province of Arbil as its sector. "Korea's Zaytun Troops Mark 1st Anniversary in Iraq," *Korea Update* 16, no. 10 (31 August 2005) [article on-line] available at http://www.koreaemb.org/archive/2005/8_2/foreign/foreign1.asp; Internet; accessed 26 October 2005.

10. As of October 2005, at only three points in time were there more than 100 US KIAs: April 2004, with 135 (55 during the first battle of Fallujah and another eight during the Sadr City fight with the Mahdi militia), November 2004, with 137 (of which 71 deaths occurred during the second battle of Fallujah); and January 2005 with 107, including 31 killed in a Marine helicopter crash. See "US Troop Deaths Hit 100 Mark for Only Third Month Since the War Began," 1 February 2005 [article on-line] available at http://www.signonsandiego.com/news/world/iraq/memorial/20050201-1403-iraq-uslosses.html; Internet; accessed 26 October 2005.

11. Eric Schmitt, "US Commanders See Possible Cuts in Troops in Iraq," *New York Times,* 11 April 2005 [article on-line] available at http://www.globalpolicy.org/security/issues/iraq/occupation/2005/0411cut.htm; Internet; accessed 27 October 2005.

12. Non-American Coalition forces in Iraq totaled about 33,000.

13. Bradley Graham, "U.S. to Pull 15,000 Troops Out of Iraq," *Washington Post,* 4 February 2005, p. A01 [article on-line] available at http://www.washingtonpost.com/wp-dyn/articles/A61910-2005Feb3.html; Internet; accessed 28 October 2005; "US Forces Order of battle – 4 March 2005," 8 November 2005 [document on-line] available at http://www.globalsecurity.org/military/ops/iraq_orbat.htm; Internet; accessed 28 October 2005. For information on units extended in Iraq see "Department of Defense Announces Troop Extensions for Iraq," Department of Defense Press Release, 1 December 2004 [press release on-line] available at http://www.defenselink.mil/releases/2004/nr20041201-1741.html; Internet; accessed 20 October 2005.

14. "Numbers of US Troops in Iraq Has Risen," Associated Press, 7 October 2005 [article on-line] available at http://www.military.com/NewsContent/0,13319,78282,00.html?ESRC=army.nl; Internet; accessed 26 October 2005; Will Dunham, "US Increases to 152,000 Troops for Iraq Referendum," *Reuters,* 6 October 2005, [article on-line] available at http://www.boston.com/news/world/middleeast/articles/2005/10/06/us_increases_to_152000_troops_for_iraq_referendum?mode=PF; accessed 10 February 2005.

15. Dunham; "DoD Announces OEF/OIF Rotational Units," Department of Defense Press Release, 14 December 2004 [press release on-line] available at http://www.defenselink.mil/releases/2004/nr20041214-1823.html; Internet; accessed 30 October 2005. For example, the 3-504th Infantry, a paratrooper battalion from the 82d Airborne Division, was dispatched to reinforce II MEF for a short tour of several months in September 2005. OIF IV units deployed prior to

the referendum included the 172d Infantry Brigade (Stryker), 2d Brigade, 28th Infantry Division (Pennsylvania Army National Guard [ARNG]), 56th Cavalry Brigade, 36th Infantry Division (Mechanized) (Texas ARNG) and the 48th Infantry Brigade (Mechanized) (Georgia ARNG).

16. VandeHei; Mark Mazzetti, "US Generals Now See the Virtues of a Smaller Troop Presence in Iraq," *Los Angeles Times,* 1 October 2005, [article on-line] available at http://news.yahoo.com/s/latimests/20051001/ts_latimes/usgenerals nowseevirtuesofasmallertrooppresenceiniraq; accessed 30 October 2005.

17. *Atlas of the Middle East* (Washington, DC: National Geographic Society, 2003), 65

18. The Turkmen or Turkomen, are variously described as Turkish settlers from the 18th century, or descendents of Turkic speaking Oghuz tribesman from medieval times. The language they speak is variously described as a dialect of Turkish or related to the speech of Azerbaijani Republic in the Caucasus. The cited numbers of Turkmen in Iraq varies between 10,000 and 3 million, with the figure likely over one million. See "Iraqi Turkmen," [document on-line] available at http://www.unpo.org/member.php?arg=27; Internet; accessed 31 October 2005.

19. Kevin Benson, "'Phase IV' CFLCC Stability Operations Planning," in *Turning Victory into Success: Military Operations After the Campaign* ed. Brian DeToy (paper presented at conference sponsored by US Army Training and Doctrine Command, Fort Leavenworth, KS, 14-16 September 2004); (Fort Leavenworth: Combat Studies Institute Press, 2004), 187; "Iraq: Administrative Divisions (Population and Area)," *World Gazetteer*, [table on-line] available at http://www.world-gazetteer.com/r/r_iq.htm; accessed October 31, 2005. The latter reference was only used for geographical purposes.

20. Several provinces have honorific titles. The Province of Babil or Babylonia is named to commemorate the ancient empire of Babylonia, the ruins of whose capital, Babylon, are located in Babil. Salah-ad-Din or Saladin is named after the 12th century military leader who fought against the crusaders. Saladin was born in Tikrit, one of the major cities of Salah-ad-Din Province. Ironically, considering the Baathist treatment of that group, Saladin was a Kurd.

21. Benson, 179-206.

22. Ibid., 185-9. Benson chose California because it was roughly similar to Iraq in size. However, as was discussed in chapter 3, it was a poor choice as two of its major police forces, those of the cities of Los Angeles and San Diego, are anomalies in their proportional size compared to most other American municipal police departments.

23. Ibid., 189.

24. Ibid., 198. Using Benson's figures as guidelines, a four-battalion brigade would equate to 6250 soldiers and its support slice would be 1.4 times this strength, or 8750 resulting in 15,000 soldiers in a brigade equivalent.

25. The order of battle in January 2005 with brigade equivalents is found in table B-13, appendix B.

26. The average coalition strength between April 2003 and September 2005 was 159,065. The US land forces average was 132,850. See figure 32 for monthly strengths during that period. The methodology of this study is to look at the maximum troop density in a historical contingency operation, presuming that it is better to have the maximum needed number of troops rather than an average or minimum force size as a guideline for planning troop density.

27. "ENCL 2: Operational Graphics for the Clearance of Southwest Baghdad" (PowerPoint presentation, Disc 38 of 68), 2-17th Cavalry, 25 April 2003. Document was collected by OIF study group as primary source material during a trip to Iraq to collect archival material. Originally housed at the 35th Infantry Division Headquarters in Leavenworth, KS.

28. The decision to disband the Iraqi forces became one of the most controversial of the occupation. Bremer's immediate predecessor, Jay Garner, wanted to use the former Iraqi Ministry of Defense and Army to employ the masses of soldiers. See Jay Garner, "Iraq Revisited," in *Turning Victory into Success: Military Operations After the Campaign* ed. Brian DeToy (paper presented at conference sponsored by US Army Training and Doctrine Command, Fort Leavenworth, KS, 14-16 September 2004); (Fort Leavenworth: Combat Studies Institute Press, 2004), 265. On the other hand, the Iraqis felt that the issue was not that significant. See Anthony Cordesman, "Iraqi Force Development: An Iraqi View," 10 March 2005, 3-4 [document on-line] available at http://www.csis.org/media/csis/pubs/050310_iraqiforces.pdf; Internet; accessed 7 November 2005.

29. "Iraqi Military Reconstruction;" Iraq to Dissolve National Guard," *BBC News/Middle East*, 29 December 2004, [article on-line] available at http://news.bbc.co.uk/2/low/middle_east/4133039.stm; Internet; accessed 7 November 2005.

30. Anthony Cordesman, "Iraqi Forces Development: Can Iraqi Forces Do the Job?" 8 August 2005, 15 [document on-line] available at http://www.csis.org/media/csis/pubs/050808_iraqiforces.pdf; Internet; accessed 7 November 2005.

31. "Iraqi Military Reconstruction"; Anthony Cordesman, "Inexcusable Failure: Progress in training the Iraqi Army and Security Forces as of Mid-July 2004," 20 July 2004, 1-12 [document on-line] available at http://www.csis.org/media/csis/pubs/iraq_inexcusablefailure.pdf; Internet; accessed 7 November 2005.

32. "Iraqi Police Force Reviewed", Knight Ridder Newspapers, 23 October 2004, [article on-line] available at http://64.233.179.104/search?q=cache:VIsxfnbVwt4J:charleston.net/stories/102304/ter_23police.shtml+%22Iraqi+Police+Force+Reviewed%22&hl=en&gl=us&ct=clnk&cd=1; Internet; accessed 7 November; Walter Pincus, "U.S. Says More Iraqi Police Are Needed as Attacks Continue," *Washington Post*, 28 September 2004, p. A23 (F). At least one observer claimed that the sharp fall in police strength to indicate large-scale desertion rather than a government review. See William Kulin, "50% of Iraqi Police Have Deserted (The 50-Year Occupation)," 26 November 2004 [article on-line] available at http://www.globalsecurity.org/org/news/2004/041126-iraq.htm; Internet; accessed 3 November 2005.

33. "Iraqi Brigade Takes Control of Area, Future," 23 February 2005 [press release on-line] available at http://www.defendamerica.mil/articles/feb2005/

a022305la4.html; Internet; accessed 7 November 2005. The former 40th Brigade, Iraqi National Guard, was reflagged as the 1st Brigade, 6th Division. The 6th Division was the Iraqi army's designated Baghdad defense division.

34. Cordesman, "Iraqi Forces Development," 15.

35. VandHei; Sara Wood, "Iraqi Forces to Provide Bulk of Election Security," 2 September 2005, [article on-line] available at http://www.blackanthem.com/World/2005090208.html; Internet; accessed 3 November 2005; Elaine Grossman, "Officers Worry Iraqi Army Will Disintegrate After U.S. Draws Down," *Inside Washington Publishers,* 15 September 2005 [article on-line] available at http://www.d-n-i.net/grossman/iraqi_army_will_disintegrate.htm; Internet; accessed 26 October 2005; Josh White and Bradley Graham, "Decline in Troops' Readiness Cited," *Washington Post,* 30 September 2005, p. A12(F) [article archived online] available at http://pqasb.pqarchiver.com/washingtonpost/access/904706971. html?dids=904706971:904706971&FMT=ABS&FMTS=ABS:FT&fmac=&date=Sep+30%2C+2005&author=Josh+White+and+Bradley+Graham&desc=Decline+in+Iraqi+Troops%27+Readiness+Cited; Internet; accessed 7 November 2005; "101st's 1st BCT Takes Over Authority for Kirkuk Area Base," *This Week in Iraq,* 1, no. 12 (2 November 2005) : 1,3 [article on-line] available at http://www.mnf iraq.com/Publications/TWII/02Nov.pdf; Internet; accessed 4 November 2005.

36. Sara Wood, "Partnership Between U.S., Iraqi Logistics Forces Yielding Results, Commander Says," 12 August 2005 [press release on-line] available at http://www.defenselink.mil/news/Aug2005/20050812_2405.html; Internet; accessed 7 November 2005.

37. Cordesman, "Iraqi Forces Development," 12, 17.

38. Eric Schmitt, "Pentagon Contradicts General on Iraq Occupation Force's Size"; "Wallace Failed to Challenge Rumsfeld's False Claims about Troop Levels in Iraq, which Hume Later Echoed," 28 June 2005 [article on-line] available at http://mediamatters.org/items/200506280010; Internet; accessed 26 October 2005; see also Benson, 198. The 'too few' troops controversy gained new fuel in October 2004 when comments from former CPA Director Paul Bremer were interpreted by some media sources to mean that he felt there were too few troops in Iraq when he was there. Bremer later clarified that he meant more troops were needed immediately after the end of the Baghdad campaign. In the period from April to May 2003, Coalition forces did increase from 118,000 to 168,500. For the Bremer controversy, see "Bremer Remarks Fuel Campaign Fire," *CBS News,* 5 October 2004 [article archived on-line] available at http://www.cbsnews.com/stories/2004/10/05/iraq/main647476.shtml?CMP=ILC-SearchStories; Internet; accessed 26 October 2005. In a recent work on the Baghdad campaign, the authors emphasize the similarity of CENTCOM planning estimates with those of Shinseki. Michael R. Gordon and Bernard E Trainor, *Cobra II: The Inside Story of the Invasion and Occupation of Iraq* (New York: Pantheon Books, 2006), 103.

39. "General Abizaid Central Command Operations Update Briefing," (Central Command [CENTCOM] press briefing by CENTCOM Commander, General John Abizaid, Qatar, 30 April 2004) April 2004 [transcripts on-line] available at

http://www.defenselink.mil/transcripts/2004/tr20040430-1402.html; Internet; accessed 3 November 2005.

40. Mazzetti; Grossman.

Chapter 6
Conclusion

This work analyzed successful past contingency operations in order to determine historical trends in the troop densities of such deployments. The methodology was to use the maximum number of troops deployed in an operation as the snapshot benchmark because planning factors should be based on the maximum amount of forces ultimately needed in a contingency operation, rather than an average or minimal number. Accordingly, these factors are inherently based on the worst-case scenario for each operation studied.

The results of the analysis show clearly that past deployment strengths have been primarily based on the population of the operational area rather than its size. Additionally, while many current sources cite as a standard a minimum of 20 troops to 1000 inhabitants as the necessary ratio, the case studies of this work indicate a figure of about 13.26 troops per 1000 inhabitants provides a more historically based guideline. Moreover, the figure of 13.26 includes any other operational forces including indigenous police and military forces, as well as contractors.

This work also analyzed a sampling of the largest and most successful municipal police forces in the United States in terms of size and density. As with military forces in contingency operations, police force size has been almost exclusively based on the size of the population the force supported. The average ratio of police officers to population was 4.1 per 1000. Since troops deployed operationally for contingency operations assume police roles as an inherent part of their mission, this indicates that such a force requires a minimum of 4.1 troops per 1000 of local population to be engaged in police activities. With an overall planning factor of 13.26 troops per 1000 residents, this means about 30 percent or slightly less than one-third of the projected force in a contingency operation should be employed as police.

Forces in contingency operations are usually deployed in operational units. In this work, the brigade or its equivalent is used as the basic operational unit. The brigade equivalent, including its support slice, averaged 5909 troops. The planning factor for the number of brigades deployed is one brigade for every 483,141 inhabitants.

Table 19 summarizes the planning factors. As a useful addition, the table also includes revised planning factors, which include the Iraqi deployment as one of the historical examples from which data was drawn. If the Iraqi operation is included, the planning factor figures become slightly less dense, while the brigade equivalent size becomes slightly larger both in size and in proportion to the local inhabitants.

The planning factors provide general guidelines for future contingency operation deployments based on successful historical operations. However, each situation remains unique with its own set of variables that may or may not result in force densities higher or lower than the planning factors, and operational employment of brigade-equivalent forces of greater or lesser numbers than the factors indicate. Nevertheless, because of this work, future operational planners have a starting point for determining how many troops will be necessary to execute a contingency operation.

Table 19. Planning Factor Summary

Planning Factors	
Adjusted force planning factor	13.26 soldiers per 1000 of population
	91.82 inhabitants per soldier
Brigade-equivalent planning factor size	5909 troops
Brigade equivalent to population ratio	One brigade per 483,141 inhabitants
Proportion of force density devoted to police operations	4.1 per 1000 (30 percent of force size)
Planning Factors (including Iraq)	
Adjusted force planning factor	12.43 soldiers per 1000 of population
	98.01 inhabitants per soldier
Brigade-equivalent planning factor size	6064 troops
Brigade equivalent to population ratio	One brigade per 429,458 inhabitants

About the Author

Boston native John McGrath has worked for the United States Army in one capacity or another since 1978. A retired Army Reserve officer, Mr. McGrath served in infantry, field artillery, and logistics units, both on active duty and as a reservist. Before coming to work at the Combat Studies Institute, he worked for four years at the US Army Center of Military History in Washington, DC, as a historian and archivist. Prior to that, Mr. McGrath worked full time for the United States Army Reserve in Massachusetts for more than 15 years, both as an active duty reservist and as a civilian military technician. He also served as a mobilized reservist in 1991 in Saudi Arabia with the 22d Support Command during Operation DESERT STORM as the command historian and in 1992 at the US Army Center of Military History as a researcher and writer.

Mr. McGrath is a graduate of Boston College, holds an MA in history from the University of Massachusetts at Boston, and is currently a PhD candidate at Kansas State University. He is the author of numerous articles and military history publications. He has published several books including *Theater Logistics in the Gulf War* published by the Army Materiel Command in 1994, *The Brigade: A History* published by the US Army Combat Studies Institute (CSI) in 2005; and *Crossing the Line of Departure*, also published by CSI in 2006. He served as the general editor of the published proceedings from CSI's 2005 Military History Symposium, *An Army at War: Change in the Midst of Conflict*. Aside from a general interest in things military and historical, his areas of particular interest include modern military operations, the German army in World War II, August 1914, and the Union Army in the Civil War. He also has a keen interest in ancient history, historical linguistics, the city of Boston, and baseball.

Bibliography

"101st's 1st BCT Takes Over Authority for Kirkuk Area Base," US Army, *This Week in Iraq*, 1, no. 12 (2 November 2005) : 1,3 [article on-line] available at http://www.mnf-iraq.com/Publications/TWII/02Nov.pdf; Internet; accessed 4 November 2005.

"2000 Census: US Municipalities Over 50,000: Ranked by 2000 Population," [document on-line] available at http://www.demographia.com/db-uscity98. htm; Internet; accessed 23 September 2005.

2-17th Cavalry, "ENCL 2: Operational Graphics for the Clearance of Southwest Baghdad." (PowerPoint presentation, Disc 38 of 68), 2-17th Cavalry, 25 April 2003. Document was collected by OIF study group as primary source material during a trip to Iraq to collect archival material. Originally housed at the 35th Infantry Division Headquarters in Leavenworth, KS.

"The Armed Forces in Bosnia and Herzegovina," *EUFOR: European Union Force in Bosnia and Herzegovina* [website on-line] available at http://www. euforbih.org/bih/tchapter4.htm; Internet; accessed 18 October 2005.

The Army Almanac: A Book of Facts Concerning the Army of the United States. Washington, DC: Government Printing Office, 1950.

"Army Announces Updated Balkans Rotation Schedule," 4 December 2000 [press release on-line] available at http://www4.army.mil/ocpa/read.php?story_id_ key=1761; Internet; accessed 20 October 2005.

Army in Europe (AE) Pamphlet 525-100, *The U.S. Army in Bosnia and Herzegovina* (Heidelberg, Germany: US Army Europe, 7th Army, 2003): 22-4 [document on-line] available at http://www.fas.org/irp/doddir/army/ae-pam-525-100.pdf; Internet; accessed 17 October 2005.

"Army of Bosnia and Herzegovina: Order of Battle 1995," October 2004 [website on-line] available at http://www.vojska.net/military/bih/armija/orbat/1995/ default.asp; Internet; accessed 18 October 2005.

"Army of Republic of Srpska: Order of Battle, 1992-1995," September 2003 [website on-line] available at http://www.vojska.net/military/bih/vrs/oob/1995. asp; Internet; accessed 18 October 2005.

Atlas of the Middle East. Washington, DC: National Geographic Society, 2003.

"Background to the Conflict," *Official Site of the Kosovo Force* [website on-line] available at http://www.nato.int/kfor/kfor/intro.htm; Internet; accessed 19 October 2005.

Benson, Kevin. "'Phase IV' CFLCC Stability Operations Planning." In *Turning Victory into Success: Military Operations After the Campaign* edited by Brian DeToy (paper presented at conference sponsored by US Army Training and Doctrine Command, Fort Leavenworth, KS, 14-16 September] 2004); Fort Leavenworth, KS: Combat Studies Institute Press, 2004.

Birtle, Andrew J. *U.S. Army Counterinsurgency and Contingency Operations Doctrine, 1860-1941.* Washington, DC: Center of Military History, 1998.

"Bosnia and Herzegovina." *CIA World Factbook* [document on-line] available at http://www.cia.gov/cia/publications/factbook/geos/bk.html; Internet; accessed 13 October 2005.

"Bosnia's Next Five Years: Dayton and Beyond." November 2000 [document on-line] available at http://www.usip.org/pubs/specialreports/sr001103.html; Internet; accessed 17 October 2005.

"Bosnia's Stalled Police Reform: No Progress, No EU," *International Crisis Group Europe Report,* no. 164, 6 September 2005 [report on-line] available at http://www.crisisgroup.org/home/index.cfm?id=3645&l=1; Internet; accessed 18 October 2005.

Boston Police Department official website [on-line] available at http://www. cityofboston.gov/police/district.asp; Internet; accessed 30 August 2005.

"Bremer Defends Disbanding Iraqi Army—Ex U.S. Administrator: Immediate Postwar Decisions were Correct," *MSNBC/Reuters,* 12 January 2005 [article on-line] available at http://www.msnbc.msn.com/id/6815732; Internet; accessed 20 January 2005.

"Bremer Remarks Fuel Campaign Fire," *CBS News,* 5 October 2004 [article archived on-line] available at http://www.cbsnews.com/stories/2004/10/05/iraq/main647476.shtml?CMP=ILC-SearchStories; Internet; accessed 26 October 2005.

"Brief History of Australia's Participation in the Occupation of Japan, 1945-1952," *British Commonwealth Occupation Forces National Council* [document on-line] available at http://www.bradprint.com.au/bcof/history.html; Internet; accessed 11 October 2005.

"Brief History of the Chicago Police Department," *Chicago Historical Information,* August 1997 [document on-line] available at http://www.chipublib.org/004chicago/timeline/policedept.html; Internet; accessed 28 September 2005.

"Briefing by the Defence Secretary, Mr. George Robertson and the Deputy Chief of the Defence Staff (Commitments), Air Marshall Sir John Day," (press **briefing at the London Ministry of Defence, 26 May 1999) [press briefing** on-line] available at http://www.kosovo.mod.uk/brief260599.htm; Internet; accessed 19 October 2005.

"Brigade of Gurkhas History," [document on-line] available at http://www.army. mod.uk/linked_files/gurkhas/The_World_Wars_and_the_subsequent_hiso ry.doc; Internet; accessed 6 September 2005.

Brown, John S. "Numerical Considerations in Military Occupations," Army (April 2006), [document on-line]; http://www.ausa.org/webpub/DeptArmyMaga-zine.nsf/byid/KHYL-6MYKGY, accessed 16 June 2006.

Budiansky, Stephen. "Formula for How Many Troops We Need," *Washington Post,* 9 May 2004, p. B04 [article on-line] available at http://www.spokes manreview.com/breaking-news-story.asp?submitdate=2004510151143; Internet; accessed 13 January 2005.

California Highway Patrol [website on-line] available at www.chp.ca.gov; Internet; accessed 17 August 2005.

Cameron, Robert. "There and Back Again: Constabulary Training and

Organization, 1946-1950." In *Armed Diplomacy: Two Centuries of American Campaigning* (paper presented at conference sponsored by US Army Training and Doctrine Command, Fort Leavenworth, KS, 5-7 August 2003); Fort Leavenworth, KS: Combat Studies Institute Press, 2003.

Carafano, James J. "Swords into Plowshares: Postconflict Arms Management," *Military Review* 77, no. 6 (November/December 1997).

Chicago Police Department official website [on-line] available at http://egov. cityofchicago.org/city/webportal/portalEntityHomeAction.do?BV_SessionI D=@@@@@0399460732.1133145217@@@@@&BV _EngineID=cccdaddg fekemficefecelldffhdfgm.0&entityName=Police&entityNameEnumValue=3 3; Internet; accessed 27 November 2005.

Coates, John. *Suppressing Insurgency: An Analysis of the Malayan Emergency, 1948-1954*. Boulder, CO: Westview Press, 1992.

Cohen, Theodore. *Remaking Japan: The American Occupation as New Deal*. Edited by Herbert Passin. New York: Free Press, 1988.

"Conservative Critiques of the War, Part I: Introduction," 11 January 2005. *The Adventures of Chester*. [web log on-line] available at http://adventuresof chester.blogspot.com/2005/01/conservative-critiques-of-war-part-i.html; Internet; accessed 13 January 2005.

Cordesman, Anthony. "Inexcusable Failure: Progress in Training the Iraqi Army and Security Forces as of mid-July 2004," *Center for Strategic and International Studies*, 20 July 2004; [document on-line] available at http://www. csis.org/media/csis/pubs/iraq_inexcusablefailure.pdf; Internet; accessed 7 November 2005.

_____. "Iraqi Force Development: An Iraqi View," *Center for Strategic and International Studies*, 10 March 2005, 3-4; [document on-line] available at "http://www.csis.org/media/csis/pubs/050310_iraqiforces.pdf; Internet; accessed 7 November 2005.

_____. "Iraqi Forces Development: Can Iraqi Forces Do the Job?" *Center for Strategic and International Studies*. 8 August 2005; [document on-line] available at http://www.csis.org/media/csis/pubs/050808_iraqiforces.pdf; Internet; accessed 7 November 2005.

Cordesman, Anthony and William D. Sullivan, "Iraqi Force Development in 2006." (Washington, DC: Center for Strategic and International Studies, June 2006), 32, 83, 109.

Cordner, Gary. "State Police in the United States-December 2003;" [document on-line] available at http://www.csg.org/NR/rdonlyres/ ex 4lwhthmpcxm4pldsgebvlym4nlyprx4lg3wajkuzsoa4omqkxlt37bctcqp2kc7 fdqr5qttjnubt5gcuhr6mpknjb/State+Police+stats.pdf; Internet; accessed 26 August 2005.

Correspondence Relating to the War with Spain including the Insurrection in the Philippine Islands and the China Relief Expedition, April 15, 1898 to July 30, 1902. 2 vols. Washington, DC: US Army Center of Military History, 1993.

Crane, Conrad C. and W. Andrew Terrill. *Reconstructing Iraq: Insights,*

Challenges and Missions for Military Forces in a Post-Conflict Scenario. Carlisle Barracks, PA: Strategic Studies Institute, US Army War College, February, 2003.

"The Crime Beat: LAPD Thumbnail." *Covering Crime and Justice*; [web log on-line] available at http://www.justicejournalism.org/crimeguide/chapter01/sidebars/chap01_xside8.html; Internet; accessed 15 September 2005.

"Crime Rates for Selected Large Cities, 2002." *Infoplease*; [table on-line] available at http://www.infoplease.com/ipa/A0004902.htm; Internet; accessed 16 September 2005.

"Department of Defense Announces Troop Extensions for Iraq," Department of Defense News Release No. 1232-04, 1 December 2004; [document on-line] available at http://www.defenselink.mil/releases/2004/nr20041201-1741.html; Internet; accessed 30 October 2005.

"DoD Announces OEF/OIF Rotational Units." Department of Defense News Release No. 1289-04, 14 December 2004; [document on-line] available at http://www.defenselink.mil/releases/2004/nr20041214-1823.html; Internet; accessed 30 October 2005.

Department of the Army. FM 7-30, *The Infantry Brigade*, with Change 1 dated 31 October 2000. Washington: DC, Department of the Army, 3 October 1995.

Department of the Army. FM 100-23 [3-07.3] *Peace Operations*. Washington, DC: Department of the Army, December 1994.

Department of the Army. FM 101-10-1/2, *Staff Officers' Field Manual: Organizational, Technical, and Logistical Data Planning Factors (Volume 2)*. Washington, DC: Department of the Army, 1987, with change 1 (17 July 1990).

Dobbins, James, John G. McGinn, Keith Crane, Seth G. Jones, Rollie Lal, Andrew Rathmell, Rachel Swanger, and Anga Timilsina. *America's Role in Nation-Building: From Germany to Iraq*. MR-1753. Santa Monica, CA:Rand, 2003; [book on-line] available at http://www.rand.org/publications/MR/MR1753/; Internet; accessed 27 January 2005.

Drum, Kevin. "Not Enough Troops in Iraq?" *Washington Monthly*, 9 January 2005. Political Animal; [column on-line] available at http://www.washingtonmonthly.com/archives/individual/2005_01/005422.php; Internet; accessed on 14 January 2005.

Dunham, Will. "US Increases to 152,000 Troops for Iraq Referendum." *Reuters*, 6 October 2005; [article on-line] available at http://news.yahoo.com/s/nm/20051006/ts_nm/iraq_usa_troops_dc ; Internet; accessed 26 October 2005.

Fattig, Paul. "Iraq War Commander Defends Bush Policy: Retired Gen. Franks Praises the President's Leadership; Pro-Kerry Vets Cite 'Distortion." *Medford* (OR) *Mail Tribune*, 12 October 2004; [article on-line] available at http://www.mailtribune.com/archive/2004/1012/local/stories/02local.htm; Internet; accessed on 10 January 2005.

"The First Year of the Occupation," in *Occupation Forces in Europe Series, 1945-1946,* vol. 1 (Office of the Chief Historian, European Command, 1947).

Frederiksen, Oliver J. *The American Military Occupation of Germany 1945-1953.*

Darmstadt, Germany: Historical Division, Headquarters, US Army Europe, 1953.

Garamone, James. "Ending War, Enforcing Peace in Bosnia." *American Forces Press Services* 2 December 2004 [press release on-line] available at http://www.defenselink.mil/news/Dec2004/n12022004_2004120208.html; Internet; accessed 17 October 2005.

Garner, Jay. "Iraq Revisited." In *Turning Victory into Success: Military Operations After the Campaign,* edited by Brian DeToy. (Paper presented at conference sponsored by US Army Training and Doctrine Command, Fort Leavenworth, KS, 14-16 September 2004); Fort Leavenworth, KS: Combat Studies Institute Press, 2005.

Garson, G. David and Irvin B. Vann. "Chapter 1: Benefits of Geographic Information Systems," *Geographic Information Systems for Small and Medium Law Enforcement Jurisdictions: Strategies and Effective Practices.* North Carolina Governor's Crime Commission, North Carolina Criminal Justice Analysis Center, February 2001. [document on-line] available at http://www.gcc.state.nc.us/gispage/chapter1.htm; Internet; accessed 25 January 2005.

Gates, Daryl F. with Diane K. Shah. *Chief: My Life in the L.A.P.D.* New York: Bantam Books, 1992.

"General Abizaid Central Command Operations Update Briefing." *News Transcript.* 23 April 2004; [document on-line] available at http://www.defenselink.mil/transcripts/2004/tr20040430-1402.html; Internet; accessed 3 November 2005.

"General Keane Press Briefing on Plans to Rotate Forces in Iraq," (Pentagon press briefing by acting Army chief of staff and other military officials, Washington, DC, 23 July 2003) July 2003 [transcripts on-line] available at http://www.globalsecurity.org/military/library/news/2003/07/mil-030723-dod03.htm; Internet; accessed 27 October 2005.

Gibson, Campbell. "Population of the 100 Largest Cities and Other Urban Places in the United States: 1790 to 1990." Washington, DC: US Census Bureau, June 1998. [document on-line] available at http://www.census.gov/population/www/documentation/twps0027.html#taba; Internet; accessed 16 September 2005.

Gordon, Michael R. and Bernard E. Trainor. *Cobra II: The Inside story of the Invasion and Occupation of Iraq.* New York: Pantheon Books, 2006.

Gordon, Michael R. "How Much is Enough–US Troops in Iraq," *New York Times,* 30 May 2003 [article on-line] available at http://www.nytimes.com/2003/05/30/international/worldspecial/30CND-GORDON.html?ex=1142744400&en=477bda6fcdb54c89&ei=5070; Internet; accessed 10 January 2005.

Gott, Kendall. *Mobility, Vigilance, and Justice: The US Army Constabulary in Germany, 1941-1953.* Global War on Terrorism Occasional Paper 11. Fort Leavenworth, KS: Combat Studies Institute Press, 2005.

Graham, Bradley. "U.S. to Pull 15,000 Troops Out of Iraq," *Washington Post,* 4 February 2005, p. A01 [article on-line] available at http://www.washing

tonpost.com/wp-dyn/articles/A61910-2005Feb3.html; Internet; accessed 28 October 2005.

Grossman, Elaine. "Officers Worry Iraqi Army Will Disintegrate After U.S. Draws Down," *Inside Washington Publishers,* 15 September 2005 [article on-line] available at http://www.d-n-i.net/grossman/iraqi_army_will_disintegrate. htm; Internet; accessed 26 October 2005.

Hennefer, Thomas E. "Use of Private Military Corporations to Supplement Traditional American Ground Forces." In *An Army at War: Change in the Midst of Conflict, Proceedings of the Combat Studies Institute 2005 Military History Symposium,* edited by John J. McGrath. Fort Leavenworth, KS: Combat Studies Institute Press, 2005.

Hersh, Michael and John Barry. "Drawing down in Iraq: Drastic Troop Cuts are in the Pentagon's Secret Plans," *Newsweek,* 8 August 2005 [article on-line] available at http://www.msnbc.msn.com/id/8770418/site/newsweek/; Internet; accessed 24 October 2005.

Hirschman, Charles. "The Society and Its Environment." In *Malaysia: A Country Study,* edited by Frederica M. Bunge. Washington, DC: Headquarters, Department of the Army, 1984.

Historical Division, European Command, US Army. "The Evolution of the Occupation Forces in Europe." Occupation Forces in Europe Series. Frankfurt, Germany: US Army, 1948.

Historical Division, European Command, US Army, "The Third Year of the Occupation, First Quarter: 1 July-30 September 1947." Occupation Forces in Europe Series, 1947-48. Frankfurt, Germany: US Army, 1947.

Historical Division, European Command, US Army. "The Third Year of the Occupation, First Quarter." Occupation Forces in Europe Series. Vol. 1. Frankfurt, Germany: US Army, 1947.

"The History of the British Army–Malaya 1950-1957," [website on-line] available at http://www.national-army-museum.ac.uk/pages/malaya.html; Internet; accessed 9 September 2005.

"The History of the British Army–National Service and the post-1945 British Army," [website on-line] available at http://www.national-army-museum. ac.uk/pages/nat-service.html; Internet; accessed 6 September 2005.

"IFOR: Participating Forces," The Balkan Conflict; [website on-line] available at http://home.wandoo.nl/tcc/balkan/ifor_forces.html; Internet; accessed 17 October 2005.

"Interview James Fallows," *PBS Frontline: The Invasion of Iraq,* 28 January 2004 [interview transcript on-line] available at http://www.pbs.org/wgbh/ pages/frontline/shows/invasion/interviews/fallows.html; Internet; accessed 10 January 2005.

"Iraq: Administrative Divisions (Population and Area)," [website on-line] available at http://www.world-gazetteer.com/r/r_iq.htm; Internet; accessed 31 October 2005.

"Iraq to Dissolve National Guard," *BBC News/Middle East,* 29 December 2004 [article on-line] available at http://news.bbc.co.uk/2/low/middle_east/4133039.stm; Internet; accessed 7 November 2005.

"Iraq-US Ground Forces End Strength," Global Security.org; [article on-line] available at http://www.globalsecurity.org/military.ops/iraq_orbat_es.html; Internet; accessed 24 October 2005.

"Iraqi Brigade Takes Control of Area, Future," US Army,. 23 February 2005 [press release on-line] available at http://www.defendamerica.mil/articles/feb2005/a022305la4.html; Internet; accessed 7 November 2005.

"Iraqi Military Reconstruction," 27 June 2005 [document on-line] available at http://www.globalsecurity.org/military/world/iraq/iraq-corps3.htm; Internet; accessed 3 November 2005.

"Iraqi Military Reconstruction: Progress Report-Monthly," 22 September 2005 [document on-line] available at http://www.globalsecurity.org/military/world/iraq/iraq-corps5.htm; Internet; accessed 3 November 2005.

"Iraqi Police Force Reviewed," Knight Ridder Newspapers, October 23, 2004; [article on-line] available at http://charleston.net/stories/102304/ter_23police.shtml; Internet; accessed 7 November 7, 2004.

"Iraqi Turkmen." [website on-line] available at http://www.unpo.org/member.php?arg=27; Internet; accessed 31 October 2005.

"Iraqi Weekly Status Report," Bureau of Near Eastern Affairs, United States Department of State; [documents on-line] available at http://www.state.gov/p/nea/rls/rpt/iraqstatus/; Internet; accessed 10 February 2006

Jackson, Robert. *The Malayan Emergency: The Commonwealth's Wars, 1948-1966.* New York: Routledge, 1991.

Jones, Seth G., Jeremy M. Wilson, Andrew Rathmell, and K. Jack Riley, "Establishing Law and Order after Conflict" (Santa Monica, CA: Rand Corporation, 2005), xiii.

Kagan, Frederick W. "Fighting the Wrong War," *The Weekly Standard* 10, no. 17, 17 January 2005. [article on-line] available at http://www.weeklystandard.com/content/public/articles/000/000/005/119jnign.asp; Internet; accessed 21 January 2005.

Kelling, George L. and William H. Sousa Jr. *Do Police Really Matter? An Analysis of the Impact of New York City's Police Reforms,* New York: Manhattan Institute for Policy Research Civic Report no. 22, December 2001 [report on-line] available at http://www.manhattan-institute.org/html/cr_22.htm; Internet; accessed 24 January 2005.

"KFOR Headquarters," September 2005 [document on-line] available at http://www.nato.int/kfor/kfor/kfor_hq.htm; Internet; accessed 19 October 2005.

"KFOR Press Update," (press briefing by Major Roland Lavoie, KFOR spokesperson in Pristina, Kosovo, 30 August 1999) [press briefing on-line] available at http://www.nato.int/kosovo/press/1999/k990830a.htm; Internet; accessed 19 October 2005.

Kidwell, Deborah C. *Public War, Private Fight: The United States and Private Military Companies.* Global War on Terrorism Occasional Paper 12. Fort Leavenworth, KS: Combat Studies Institute Press, 2005.

"Korea's Zaytun Troops Mark 1st Anniversary in Iraq," *Korea Update* 16, no. 10 (31 August 2005) [article on-line] available at http://www.koreaemb.org/ar chive/2005/8_2/foreign/foreign1.asp; Internet; accessed 26 October 2005.

"Kosovo Protection Corps," [website on-line] available at http://www.unmikon line.org/1styear/kpcorps.htm; Internet; accessed 19 October 2005.

Kulin, William. "50% of Iraqi Police Have Deserted (The 50-Year Occupation)," 26 November 2004 [article on-line] available at http://www.globalsecurity. org/org/news/2004/041126-iraq.htm; Internet; accessed 3 November 2005.

LeSage, Jon. "Cutting Car Costs." Police One.com. 21 April 2005; [website on-line] available at http://www.policeone.com/police-products/vehicle-equip-ment/articles/99939/; Internet; accessed 25 August 2005.

Linn, Brian. *Guardians of the Empire: The U.S. Army and the Pacific, 1902-1940.* Chapel Hill, NC: University of North Carolina Press, 1997.

_____. *The Philippine War, 1899-1902.* Lawrence, KS: University Press of Kansas, 2000.

Los Angeles Police Department official website [on-line] available at http://www. lapdonline.org/; Internet; accessed 10 January 2005.

Madhani, Aamer and Colin McMahon. "Iraq Says Syria is Aiding Guerillas: GI's Job: Plug Porous Border." *Chicago Tribune*, 8 January 2005, 1; [article on-line] available at http://www.chicagotribune.com/news/nationworld/chi -05010801jan08,1,2707615.story?coll=chi-newsnationworld-hed; accessed 13 January 2005.

Martinez, Jose. "Violent City Deaths Hit Historic Lows," *New York Daily News*, 2 January 2005 [article on-line] available at http://www.nydailynews.com/front/ story/267400p-229046c.html; Internet; accessed 3 January 2005.

Mazzetti, Mark. "US Generals Now See the Virtues of a Smaller Troop Presence in Iraq." *Los Angeles Times* (1 October 2005); [article on-line] available at http:// news.yahoo.com/s/latimests/20051001/ts_latimes/usgeneralsnowseevirtueso fasmallertrooppresenceiniraq; accessed 30 October 2005.

McGrath, John J. "Army Organization in the Spanish-American War." Unpublished manuscript, Washington, DC: US Army Center of Military History, 2000.

Michta, Andrew A. "Military Capabilities of the Central Europeans: What Can They Contribute to the Stabilization of Iraq?" (summary of lecture from the Eastern European Studies at the Woodrow Wilson International Center for Scholars, Washington, DC, 2003, meeting #284) [meeting report on-line] available at http://www.wilsoncenter.org/topics/pubs/MR284Michta.doc; Internet; ac-cessed 24 October 2005

"More Men on the Ground 1." 12 January 2005. *Belmont Club: History and History in the Making*; [web log on-line] available at http://belmontclub.blogspot.com/; Internet; accessed on 10 January 2005.

"More Men on the Ground 2" 13 January 2005. *Belmont Club: History and History in the Making*; [web log on-line] available at http://belmontclub.blogspot.com/; Internet; accessed on 10 January 2005.

"More Men on the Ground 3." 13 January 2005. Belmont Club: History and His-tory in the Making; [web log on-line] available at http://belmontclub.blogspot.

com/; Internet; accessed on January 10, 2005 and http://belmontclub.blogspot. com/2005/01/more-men-on-ground-3-reader-provides.html; Internet; accessed 27 January 2005.

Morton, Louis. *The Fall of the Philippines*. United States Army in World War II: The War in the Pacific. Center of Military History Publication 5-2. Washington, DC, US Army Center of Military History, 1953.

Nagl, John A. *Learning to Eat Soup with a Knife: Counterinsurgency Lessons from Malaya and Vietnam*. Rev. ed. Chicago: University of Chicago Press, 2005.

"National Service and the Post-1949 British Army." *The History of the British Army*, [document on-line] available at http://www.national-army-museum.ac.uk/pag es/nat-service.html; Internet; accessed 6 September 2005).

New York State Division of State Police official website [on-line] available at http:// www.troopers.state.ny.us/introduction/; Internet; accessed 26 August 2005.

New York Police Department official website [on-line] available at http://www. nyc.gov/html/nypd/; Internet; accessed 20 January 2005.

"Numbers of US Troops in Iraq Has Risen," Associated Press, 7 October 2005 [article on-line] available at http://www.military.com/NewsCon tent/0,13319,78282,00.html?ESRC=army.nl; Internet; accessed 26 October 2005.

Oakerson, Ronald and Shirley Svorny. "Rightsizing Los Angeles Government," *The Independent Review* 9, no. 4 (Spring 2005) : 513-528 [journal on-line] available at http://www.independent.org/pdf/tir/tir_09_4_3_oakerson.pdf; Internet; accessed 22 September 2005.

"Officers per 1000 people," [document on-line] available at http://www.poli cepay.net/officersper.asp; Internet; accessed 23 September 2005.

"Order of Battle of the United States Army World War II: European Theater of Operations" Office of the Theater Historian: Paris, 1945.

Philadelphia Police Department official website [on-line] http://www.ppdon line.org/; Internet; accessed 22 September 2005.

Pincus, Walter. "U.S. Says More Iraqi Police Are Needed as Attacks Continue," *Washington Post*, 28 September 2004, A23 (F).

Podhoretz, Norman. "The War Against World War IV." Commentary, February 2005; [web log on-line] available at http://www.commentarymagazine. com/special/A11902025_1.html; Internet; accessed 13 January 2005.

PolicePay.net website [on-line] available at http://www.policepay.net; Internet; accessed 20 January 2005.

"Polish Commander Urges Early Iraq Vote." Associated Press, 30 August 2004; [article on-line] available at http://www.wjla.com/news/stories/0804/169623.html; Internet; accessed 25 October 2005.

"Press Briefing by Brigadier General Douglas Lute" (press briefing by Brig. Gen. Douglas Lute, Commanding General, KFOR Multinational Brigade-East, Press Club, Camp Bondsteel, Kosovo) 10 October 2002, [press briefing on-line] available at http://www.tffalcon.hqusareur.army.mil/media/ press_club/pc10oct02.pdf; Internet; accessed 19 October 2005.

"Press Conference by NATO Secretary General, Jaap de Hoop Scheffer," (press conference by NATO Secretary General, Jaap de Hoop Scheffer in Pristina, Kosovo, 13 May 2005) May 2005 [press briefing on-line] available at http://www.nato.int/docu/speech/2005/s050513a.htm; Internet; accessed 19 October 2005.

Quan, Russ. "Los Angeles' Safer Communities Proposed Measure." The Back Page, 17 January 2005; [web log on-line] available at http://nitewriter1. blogspot.com/2005_01_01_nitewriter1_archive.html; Internet; accessed 22 September 2005.

Quinlivan, James T. "Force Requirements in Stability Operations," *Parameters,* 23 (Winter 1995) : 59-69.

_____. "Burden of Victory: The Painful Arithmetic of Stability Operations," *Rand Review*, 27 no. 3 (Summer 2003) 18 August 2005 [article on-line] available at http://www.rand.org/publications/randreview/issues/sum mer2003/burden.html; Internet; accessed 14 September 2005

"The Red Cars of Los Angeles," *Los Angeles: Past, Present and Future*, 15 January 2002 [document on-line] available at http://www.usc.edu/isd/archives/la/historic/ redcars/; Internet; accessed 22 September 2005.

Reynolds, Glenn. 11 January 2005; [untitled on-line posting] available at http://insta pundit.com/archives/-20374.php; Internet; accessed on 10 January 2005.

Robinson, Colin. "The U.S. Presence in Iraq: Inching toward internationalized 'peace keeping'?" 28 July 2003 [document on-line] available at http://www.cdi.org/ friendlyversion/printversion.cfm?documentID=1534; Internet; accessed 26 October 2005.

Schmitt, Eric. "Pentagon Contradicts General on Iraq Occupation Force's Size," *New York Times* (archives) 28 February 2003 [article on-line] available at http://www.globalpolicy.org/security/issues/iraq/attack/consequences/2003/ 0228pentagoncontra.htm; Internet; accessed 10 January 2005.

_____. "US Commanders See Possible Cuts in Troops in Iraq," *New York Times,* 11 April 2005 [article on-line] available at http://www.globalpolicy.org/security/ issues/iraq/occupation/2005/0411cut.htm; Internet; accessed 27 October 2005.

Schonberger, Howard. *Aftermath of War: Americans and the Remaking of Japan, 1945-1952.* Kent, OH: Kent State University Press, 1989.

Scurr, John. *The Malayan Campaign, 1948-60.* Osprey Men-at-Arms series. London: Osprey Publishing, Ltd., 1982.

"The Second Year of the Occupation," in *Occupation Forces in Europe Series, 1946-1947,* vol. 1 Office of the Chief Historian, European Command, 1947.

"The Second Year of the Occupation," in *Occupation Forces in Europe Series, 1946-1947,* vol. 5 Office of the Chief Historian, European Command, 1947.

"Selected Demographic Indicators for Japan," *National Institute of Population and Social Security Research* October 2005 [document on-line] available at http:// www.ipss.go.jp/index-e.html; Internet; accessed 10 October 2005.

Serafino, Nina M. "Peacekeeping and Related Stability Operations: Issues of U.S. Military Involvement," *Issue Brief for Congress* by the Congressional Research Service, The Library of Congress, 4 October 2004.

_____. "Combating Terrorism: Are There Lessons to be Learned from Foreign Experiences?" *Report for Congress* by the Congressional Research Service, The Library of Congress, 18 January 2002 [document on-line] available at http://fpc. state.gov/documents/organization/7957.pdf; Internet; accessed 24 January 2005.

Simon, Roger L. "January 12, 2005: Not Just John's Father;" [web log on-line] available at http://www.rogersimon.com/mt-archives/2005/01/not_just_johns/php/; Internet; accessed 13 January 2005.

Smith, Daniel. "Iraq: Descending into the Quagmire." *Global Policy Forum*, June 2003; [document on-line] available at http://www.fpif.org/papers/quagmire2003. html; Internet; accessed 9 November 2005.

Stacey, William. *US Army Border Operations in Germany, 1945-1983*. Heidelberg, Germany: Headquarters, US Army Europe and Seventh Army, 1984.

Stanton, Shelby. *Order of Battle, U.S. Army, World War II*. Novato, CA: Presidio, 1984.

Stearman, William. *The Soviet Union and the Occupation of Austria: An Analysis of Soviet Policy in Austria, 1945-1955*. Bonn, Germany: Siegler, 1961.

Stewart, Richard W. "Occupations Then and Now." In *Armed Diplomacy: Two Centuries of American Campaigning* (paper presented at conference sponsored by US Army Training and Doctrine Command, Ft. Leavenworth, KS, 5-7 August 2003); Ft. Leavenworth, KS: Combat Studies Institute Press, 2003.

"Thin Blue Line: San Diego needs more police," *San Diego Tribune* 12 December 2004 [article on-line] available at http://www.signonsandiego.com/ uniontrib/20041212/news_lz1ed12top.html; Internet; accessed 16 September 2005.

"Troop Move Will Not Reduce Korean Security, Officials Say," (press briefing by senior defense and military officials, 17 May 2004) 18 May 2004 [transcripts on-line] available at http://usinfo.state.gov/xarchives/display. html?p=washfile-english&y=2004&m=May&x=20040518135243AJesroM 8.613223e-02&t=xarchives/xarchitem.html; Internet; accessed 28 October 2005.

Tyson, Ann Scott. "Should US Draw Down Troops in Iraq?" *Christian Science Monitor*, 23 October 2003. [article on-line] available at http://www.csmoni tor.com/2003/1023/p02s02-usmi.html; Internet; accessed 26 October 2005.

United States Forces in Austria (USFA) official history website [on-line] available at http://www.usfava.com/; Internet; accessed 7 October 2005.

"US Forces Order of Battle – 4 March 2005," [document on-line] available at http://www.globalsecurity.org/military/ops/iraq_orbat.htm; Internet; accessed 28 October 2005.

"US Troop Deaths Hit 100 Mark for Only Third Month Since the War Began," Associated Press, 1 February 2005 [article on-line] available at http://www.si gnonsandiego.com/news/world/iraq/memorial/20050201-1403-iraq-usloss es.html; Internet; accessed 26 October 2005.

Van Steenwyk, Jason. "Boots on the Ground," 9 January 2005. Countercolumn: All Your Bias Belong to Us; [web log on-line] available at http://iraqnow.

blogspot.com/2005/01/boots-on-ground.html; internet; accessed 13 January 2005.

VandeHei, Jim. "Talabani Says Iraqis Could Replace Many U.S. Troops: President's Claim About Major American Withdrawal by Year's End Conflicts With White House Position," *Washington Post*, 13 September 2005, A20 [article on-line] available at http://www.washingtonpost.com/wp-dyn/content/article/2005/09/12/AR2005091201986.html; Internet; accessed 24 October 2005.

"Wallace Failed to Challenge Rumsfeld's False Claims about Troop Levels in Iraq, which Hume Later Echoed," 28 June 2005 [article on-line] available at http://mediamatters.org/items/200506280010; Internet; accessed 26 October 2005.

White, Josh and Bradley Graham, "Decline in Troops' Readiness Cited," *Washington Post*, 30 September 2005, A12(F) [article archived on-line] available at http://www.washingotnpost.com/wp=dyn/content/article/2005/09/29/AR2005092902085.htm; Internet; accessed 7 November 2005.

Whitnah, Donald R. and Edgar L. Erickson. *The American Occupation of Austria: Planning and Early Years*. Westport, CT: Greenwood Press, 1985.

Wilson, John. *Armies, Corps, Divisions, and Separate Brigades*. Army Lineage Series. Center of Military History Publication 60-7. Washington, DC: US Army Center of Military History, 1999.

_____. *Maneuver and Firepower: The Evolution of Divisions and Separate Brigades*. Washington, DC: US Army Center of Military History, 1998.

Wood, Sara. "Iraqi Forces to Provide Bulk of Election Security," 2 September 2005 [article on-line] available at http://www.blackanthem.com/World/2005090208.html; Internet; accessed 3 November 2005.

_____. "Partnership Between U.S., Iraqi Logistics Forces Yielding Results, Commander Says," 12 August 2005 [press release on-line] available at http://www.defenselink.mil/news/Aug2005/20050812_2405.html; Internet; accessed 7 November 2005.

Wright, Robin and Thomas E. Ricks. "Bremer Criticizes Troop Levels: Ex-Overseer of Iraq says U.S. Effort was Hampered Early On." *Washington Post* 5 October 2004, A1; [article on-line] available at http://www.washingtonpost.com/wp-dyn/articles/A7053-2004Oct4.html; Internet; accessed on 20 January 2005.

Ziemke, Earl F. *The U.S. Army in the Occupation of Germany, 1944-1946*. Army Historical Series. Center of Military History Publication 30-6.Washington, DC: US Army Center of Military History, 1970.

Zink, Harold. *The United States in Germany, 1944-1955*. Princeton: Van Nostrand, 1957.

Appendix A.
Table 1. Troop Density Data

Area/Item	Military Forces (at max.)	Pop. (in 1000s)	Area (sq mi) (in 1000s)	Pop. Density (per sq mil)	Per Area (troop per sq mi)	Per Pop.(1 soldier per x # pop.)	Troops Per 1000 pop.
Philippines, 1899-1901							
Maximum October 1900	68,816	7,000.0	115.0	60.9	0.60	101.70	9.80
Northern Luzon October 1900	25,000	2,000.0	30.0	66.7	0.83	80.00	12.50
Germany, 1945-50							
Planned Army-type	285,000				6.25	66.70	15.00
Planned Police-type	203,000				4.45	93.60	10.68
Planned Constab-ulary	38,000				0.83	500.00	2.00
Actual one year June 1946	299,264	19,000.0	45.6	416.7	6.56	63.50	15.70
Actual two years June 1947	117,224				2.57	162.10	6.20
Adj. two years (includes indig.)	121,224				2.66	156.70	6.38
Actual Constab-ulary June 1947	33,333				0.73	570.01	1.75
							(continued on next page)

163

Table 1. Troop Density Data

Area/Item	Military Forces	Pop (in 1000s)	Area (in 1000s)	Pop. Density	Per Area	Per Pop.	Troops Per 1000 pop
Austria, 1945-49							
Planned	73,000				11.77	17.78	56.25
Actual two years June 1947	11,345	1,297.0	62.00	209.30	1.83	114.39	8.70
Adj. two years (includes indig.)	17,345				2.80	74.80	13.37
Japan, 1945-48							
Planned	600,000				4.20	120.25	8.32
Maximum Dec 1945	354,675				2.48	203.42	4.90
Adj. max. (including indig.)	448,675	72,147.0	142.86	505	3.14	160.80	6.20
One year Aug 1946	192,236				1.35	375.30	2.66
Commonwealth forces Aug 1946	40,236	20,000.0	22.00	909.1	1.83	497.07	2.01
Japanese police Dec 1945	94,000	72,147.0	142.86	505	0.66	767.52	1.30
Malaya, 1948-60							
Max. April 1952	30,000				0.59	161.90	6.18
Adj. (including indig.)	120,000	4,856.0	50.90	95.5	2.36	40.50	24.70

(continued on next page)

Table 1. Troop Density Data

Area/Item	Military Forces	Pop (in 1000s)	Area (in 1000s)	Pop. Density	Per Area	Per Pop.	Troops Per 1000 pop
Bosnia, 1995-96							
IFOR 1995-96	60,000				3.04	66.70	15.00
SFOR 1996-99	30,000				1.52	133.30	7.50
SFOR adj. for inter-national police	31,721	4,000.0	19.74	202.6	1.61	126.10	7.90
Kosovo, 1999	41,618	1,9700.0	4.20	468.6	9.90	47.33	21.10
Iraq, 2003-05							
Planned	300,000				1.79	85.00	11.76
Planned (adj. tooth-to-tail)	146,139				0.87	174.49	5.73
Actual max.Jan 2005	184,500	25,500.0	167.62	152.1	1.10	138.21	7.24
Adj. max. (includes contrac-or)	262,500				1.57	97.14	10.29
Baghdad, 2003-05							
Planned (adjusted)	48,000	6,200.0	.028	21,878.6	169.37	129.17	7.74
Actual (Jan 2005)	56,000				197.60	110.70	9.00
Avg. of actual deploy-ments						113.44	10.76
(continued on next page)							

165

Table 1. Troop Density Data

Area/Item	Military Forces	Pop (in 1000s)	Area (in 1000s)	Pop. Density	Per Area	Per Pop.	Troops Per 1000 pop
Adj. avg. (including indig. and other forces)	Troop Density Planning Factors					91.82	13.26
Adj.avg. including Iraq	Troop Density Planning Factors (Including Iraq)					98.01	12.43
Average municipal police forces					60.9	248.12	4.10

166

Table 2. Operational Forces

	Brigade Equivalent Size	Maximum No. of Brigade-equivalents (actual brigades deployed)	Maximum No. of Brigade-equivalents (actual brigades plus other operational forces)	Population Density per Brigade	Population Density per Brigade for the Total Force	Area Density per Brigade (sq mi) (actual brigades deployed)	Area Density per Brigade (sq mi) (total force deployed)
Philippines	3583	19.20	19.20	368,421	368,421	5990	5990
Germany one year	11,971	25.00	25.00	760,000	760,000	1824	1824
Austria	5673	2.00	3.00	648,850	432,567	3100	2066
Japan	7389	48.00	60.72	1,503,063	1,188,192	2977	2353
Malaya	3000	10.00	40.00	485,600	121,400	5085	1271
Bosnia IFOR	6000	10.00	10.00	400,000	400,000	1974	1974
Kosovo	8324	5.00	5.00	394,000	394,000	841	841
Police forces	1333			200,550	200,550		
Average	5909			595,061	483,141	3113	2706

167

Appendix B. Compendium of Tables

Note: This appendix consolidates several tables referred to in the notes.

Table 1. US Troops in Germany on V-E Day, May 1945

Infantry divisions (41)	1st, 2d, 3d, 4th, 5th, 8th, 9th, 26th, 28th, 29th, 30th, 35th, 36th, 42d, 44th, 45th, 63d, 65th, 69th, 70th, 71st, 75th, 76th, 78th, 79th, 80th, 83d, 84th, 86th, 87th, 89th, 90th, 94th, 95th, 97th, 99th, 100th, 102d, 103d, 104th, 106th
Armored divisions (15)	2d, 3d, 4th, 5th, 6th, 7th, 8th, 9th, 10th, 11th, 12th, 13th, 14th, 16th, 20th
Airborne divisions (3)	17th, 82d, 101st
Corps headquarters (15)	III, V, VI, VII, VIII, XII, XIII, XV, XVI, XVIII (Airborne), XIX, XX, XXI, XXII, XXIII
Army headquarters (5)	1st, 3d, 7th, 9th, 15th
Army group headquarters (2)	6th, 12th

Table 2. US Initial Troop Deployment, Japan 1945

Infantry divisions (ID) (12)	Americal, 1st Cav, 24th, 25th, 27th, 32d, 33d, 41st, 43d, 77th, 81st, 97th, 98th
Marine divisions (2)	2d, 5th
Airborne divisions (1)	11th
Regimental combat teams (RCTs)(3)	112th Cav, 158th, 4th Marine
Corps headquarters (7)	I, IX, X, IX, XI, XIV, V (Amphibious)
Army headquarters (2)	6th, 8th
Cav= cavalry organized as infantry	

Table 3. US Forces Downsizing, Japan 1945-46

Date	Inactivated	Redeployed
October 1945		43d, 77th IDs
December 1945	41st ID	XIV Corps, Americal Division, 27th ID
January 1946	6th Army, X Corps, 81st ID, 112th Cav, 158th RCT	V Amphibious Corps, 4th Marine Regiment
February 1946	32d, 33d, 98th IDs, 5th Marine Division	
March 1946	XI Corps, 77th, 97th IDs	
June 1946		2d Marine Division

Table 4. British and Commonwealth Order of Battle, Malayan Emergency

Unit (only battalions and above shown) Note: units listed in figure 9 are spelled out below	Deployment Dates	Remarks (Note: unit abbreviations found in this column are indicated in the far left column)
Headquarters Units		
HQ, 17th Gurkha Division	Feb 1950–Jul 1960	Organized to take control of the Gurkha brigades in Malaya; combined with South Malaya district (Sept 1952); redesignated upon Malayan independence as 17th Gurkha Division/Overseas Commonwealth Land Forces (Malaya); controlled at various times 26th, 48th, 63rd, 99th Gurkha brigades; operated primarily in northern Malaya
HQ, 1st Federation Division	1952-60	Operated primarily in southern Malaya
HQ, 2d Guards Brigade	Oct 1948–Jul 1950	Redesignated as the 18th Infantry Brigade (Jul 1950); subordinate units: 3/GG, 2d Cold, 2d Scots Gd
HQ, 48th Gurkha Brigade	Dec 1949–Jul 1960	Formed to control Gurkha battalions in Johore sub-district
HQ, 3d Commando Brigade	Apr 1950–Dec 1951	Subordinate units: 40, 42, 45th Commando (RM)
HQ, 26th Gurkha Brigade	Apr 1950–Jul 1960	Arrived from Hong Kong; subordinate units: 1 Cam, 2/6 GR, 2/10 GR
HQ, 63d Gurkha Brigade	Jul 1950–Jul 1960	Formed to command Gurkha battalions
HQ, 18th Infantry Brigade	Jul 1950–Dec 1956	Brigade disbanded (Dec 1956)
		(continued on next page)

172

Table 4. British and Commonwealth Order of Battle, Malayan Emergency

Unit	Deployment Dates	Remarks
HQ, 99th Gurkha Brigade	Sep 1952-Jul 1960	
HQ, 28th Commonwealth Brigade	Sep 1955-Jul 1960	Reformed in Malaya after service in Korea; subordinate units: British: 1/RSF, 1/RLincs, 1/Loyal, 1/3 EA, 1 Squadron, 15/19 Hussars, 11 Field Squadron. Royal Engineers; Australian: 1/RAR, 2/RAR, 3/ RAR, 105 Battery, Royal Australian Artillery, 100 Battery, Royal Australian Artillery 104 Battery, Royal Australian Artillery. New Zealand: 1/NZ
HQ, 1st Federation Brigade	1952-60	
HQ, 2d Federation Brigade	1952-60	
British Units		
1st Battalion, Kings Own Yorkshire Light Infantry (1 KOYLI)	April 1948-Aug 1951	Penang; redesignated from 2d Battalion, KOYLI, Nov 1948; replaced by 1 Manchester
1st Battalion, Devonshire Regiment (1 Devonshire)	Jun 1948-Feb 1951	1948: Johore sub-district (Singapore?); not replaced
1st Battalion, Seaforth Highlanders (1 Seaforth)	Jun 1948-Apr 1951	Amalgamated with 2d Battalion, Seaforth Higlanders, Oct 1948; in Singapore initially; 1948: Johore sub-district ; under 63d Gurkha Brigade (Dec 1950-Apr 1951); replaced by 1 Gordon Highlanders

(continued on next page)

Table 4. British and Commonwealth Order of Battle, Malayan Emergency

Unit	Deployment Dates	Remarks
26th Field Regiment, Royal Artillery (26 RA)	Jun 1948-Apr 1951	Operating as infantry; 1948: Central sub-district; replaced by 25 RA
1st Battalion, Royal Inniskilling Fusiliers (1 RIF)	Aug 1948-Aug 1949	Replaced by 1st Green Howards
3d Battalion, Grenadier Guards (3 GG)	Oct 1948-Jul 1949	Under 2d Guards Brigade; replaced by 1 Suffolk
2d Battalion, Coldstream Guards(2 Cold)	Oct 1948-Jul 1950	Under 2d Guards Brigade; replaced by 1 Worcester
2d Battalion, Scots Guards (2 Scots Gd)	Oct 1948-Mar 1951	Under 2d Gds Brigade (Oct 1948-Jul 1950), 18th Infantry Brigade (Jul 1950-Mar 1951); replaced by 1 Royal West Kent
1st Battalion, Suffolk Regiment (1 Suffolk)	Jul 1949-Jan 1953	Replaced 3 Gren Gds; replaced by 1 Somerset; under 18th Infantry Brigade
1st Battalion, Green Howards (1Green Howards)	Aug 1949-Dec 1952	Replaced 1st RIF; not replaced
40th Commando, Royal Marines (40 CDO [RM])	Aug 1949-May 1952	Under 3d Commando Brigade
1st Battalion, Cameronians (1 Cam)	Mar 1950-May 1953	Under 26th Gurkha Brigade; replaced by 1 East Yorkshire; operating in Labis (N. Johore) early 1953

(continued on next page)

Table 4. British and Commonwealth Order of Battle, Malayan Emergency

Unit	Deployment Dates	Remarks
13/18th Hussars	Jun 1950-Jul 1953; (1 squad Sep 1957) Aug 1958-Jul 1960	Replaced by 11th Hussars (1953); replaced 1 Kings Dragoon Gds (1958)
42d Commando, Royal Marines (42 CDO (RM))	Jun 1950-Jun 1953	Under 3d Commando Brigade
45th Commando, Royal Marines (45 CDO (RM))	Jun 1950-Mar 1952	Under 3d Commando Brigade
1st Battalion, Worcestershire Regiment (1 Worc)	Jul 1950-Jul 1953	Replaced 2 Cold; replaced by 1 West Yorkshire; under 18th Infantry Brigade
1st Battalion, Queen's Own Royal West Kent Regiment (1 West Kent)	Mar 1951-Mar 1954	Replaced 2 Scots Gds; replaced by 1 Hampshire; under 18th Infantry Brigade
1st Battalion, Manchester Regiment (1 Manchester)	Aug 1951-Apr 1954	Penang; replaced by 1st RSF; 18th Infantry Brigade
25th Field Regiment, Royal Artillery (25 RA)	Apr 1951-May 1956	May have been only a battery; replaced by 48th RA
1st Battalion, Gordon Highlanders (1 Gordon Highlanders)	Apr 1951-Mar 1954	Singapore; under 63d Gurkha Brigade; replaced 1st Seaforth; replaced by 1st Queens Royal Regiment

(continued on next page)

Table 4. British and Commonwealth Order of Battle, Malayan Emergency

Unit	Deployment Dates	Remarks
12th Royal Lancers (12 Lancers)	Sep 1951–Jan 1955	Replaced 4th Hussars; replaced by 15/19th Hussars
1st Battalion, Somerset Light Infantry (1 Somerset)	Jan 1953–Sep 1955	Replaced 1st Suffolk; replaced by 1st Lincoln
1st Battalion, East Yorkshire Regiment (1 East Yorkshire)	Apr 1953–Dec 1955	Replaced 1 Cam; replaced by 1 SWB; under 26th Gurkha Brigade
1st Battalion, Prince of Wale's Own (West Yorkshire) Regiment (1 West Yorkshire)	Jul 1953–Mar 1955	Replaced 1st Worcestershire
11th Hussars	Jul 1953–Aug 1956	Replaced 13/18th Hussars; replaced by 1st Kings Dragoon Gds
1st Battalion, Hampshire Regiment (1st Hampshire)	Jan 1954–Aug 1956	Replaced 1st West Kent; replaced by 1st Rifle Bde; under 18th Infantry Brigade
1st Battalion, Queen's Royal Regiment (West Surrey) (1 Queen's Royal)	Mar 1954–Feb 1957	Replaced 1st Gordon Highlanders
1st Royal Scots Fusiliers (1 RSF)	Apr 1954–May 1957	Under 28th Commonwealth Brigade; Penang
2d Battalion, Royal Welch Fusiliers (2 RWF)	Aug 1954–Aug 1957	
15/19th King's Royal Hussars (15/19 Hussars)	Aug 1954–Jun 1957	Replaced 4th Hussars; under Malaya Command; one squadron (company) under 28th Commonwealth Bde
		(continued on next page)

Table 4. British and Commonwealth Order of Battle, Malayan Emergency

Unit	Deployment Dates	Remarks
1st Battalion, King's Own Scottish Borderers (1 KOSB)	Aug 1955-Aug 1958	Under 1st Federation Brigade, 1st Federation Div (1957)
1st Battalion, Royal Lincolnshire Regiment (1 Lincolnshire)	Oct 1955-Jun 1958	Replaced 1 Somerset (Oct 1955); replaced 1/6th GR (Nov 1956); under 28th Commonwealth Bde
1st Battalion, South Wales Borderers (1 SWB)	Oct 1955-May 1958	Replaced 1st East Yorkshire; under 26th Gurkha Bde
1st Battalion, Rifle Brigade (1 Rifle Brigade)	Apr 1956-Oct 1957	Replaced 1 Hampshire
48th Field Regiment, Royal Artillery (48 RA)	May 1956-Jun 1960	
1st King's Dragoon Guards (1 Kings Drag Gds)	Jun 1956-Dec 1958	Replaced 11 Hussars; replaced by 13/18th Hussars
1st Battalion, Loyal Regiment (North Lancashire) (1 Loyal)	May 1957-Jan 1960	Under 28th Commonwealth Brigade
1st Battalion, Cheshire Regiment (1 Cheshire)	Apr 1958-Jul 1960	
1st Battalion, Sherwood Foresters (1 SF)	Jun 1958-Jul 1960	
1st Battalion, 3d East Anglian Regiment (16th/ 44th Foot) (1/3 EA)	Dec 1959-Jul 1960	Under 28th Commonwealth Brigade
22d Special Air Service Regiment	Oct 1950-58	Formed as Malayan Scouts; redesignated 22d Special Air Service Regiment (SAS) 1952; later redesignated SAS Regiment (without any numerical designation)
		(continued on next page)

Table 4. British and Commonwealth Order of Battle, Malayan Emergency

Unit	Deployment Dates	Remarks
Gurkha Units		
1st Battalion, 2d Gurkha Rifles (1/2 GR)	May 1948-Apr 1960	1948: Johore sub-district; southern sub-district (Dec 1949); 26th Gurkha Brigade (Dec 1950); 99th Gurkha Brigade (Apr 1953-Apr 1960)
1st Battalion, 6th Gurkha Rifles (1/6 GR)	May1948-Nov 1956; May 1958-60	In 1948 in northern sub-district; under 48th Gurkha Brigade (Sep 1949-Nov 1956); replaced by 1 Lincolnshire (1956)
2d Battalion, 2d Gurkha Rifles (2/2 GR)	May 1948-Sep 1953; Apr 1957-Jul 1960	In 1948 in northern sub-district; under 26th Gurkha Brigade (Dec 1950-Apr 1953; Apr 1957-Apr 1960); 48th Gurkha Brigade (Apr-Sep 1953); 99th Gurkha Brigade (Apr-Jul 1960)
2d Battalion, 6th Gurkha Rifles (2/6 GR)	May 1948-Oct 1948; Apr 1950-Jul 1960	1948: central sub-district; under 26th Gurkha Brigade (Apr 1950-Apr 1960)
1st Battalion, 7th Gurkha Rifles (1/7 GR)	May 1948-Apr 1959	1948: central sub-district converted to an artillery battalion 1948; converted back to infantry Jun 1949; under 48th Gurkha Brigade (Dec 1950-Apr 1953); 53d Gurkha Brigade (Apr 1953-Apr 1959)
2d Battalion, 7th Gurkha Rifles (2/7 GR)	May 1948-Apr 1954; Feb 1957-Jul 1960	1948: central sub-district; converted to an artillery battalion 1948; converted back to infantry Jun 1949; under 48th Gurkha Brigade (Dec 1950); 99th Gurkha Brigade (Feb 1957-Jul 1960)
		(continued on next page)

Table 4. British and Commonwealth Order of Battle, Malayan Emergency

Unit	Deployment Dates	Remarks
1st Battalion, 10th Gurkha Rifles (1/10 GR)	Jan 1948–Apr 1953; Apr–Jul 1960	1948: Johore sub-district; under 48th Gurkha Brigade (Dec 1949–Apr 1953;); Malaya Command (Apr 1953–Apr 1954); 63d Gurkha Brigade (Apr–Jul 1960)
2d Battalion, 10th Gurkha Rifles (2/10 GR)	Apr 1950–Jul 1960	Under 26th Gurkha Brigade (Apr 1950–Ap 1957); Federal Brigade (Malaya) (Apr 1957–Apr 1960); 63d Gurkha Brigade (Apr–Jul 1960).
Commonwealth Units		
1st Battalion, Malay Regiment (1/Malay Regiment)	Jun 1948–Jul 1960	1948: northern sub-district
2d Battalion, Malay Regiment (2/Malay Regiment)	Jun 1948–Jul 1960	1948: northern sub-district
3d Battalion, Malay Regiment (3/Malay Regiment)	1948-60	Battalion raised in 1948
1st (Nyasaland) Battalion, Kings African Rifles (1/ KAR)	Dec 1951–Mar 1953	Under northern command
4th Battalion, Malay Regiment (4/Malay Regiment)	1952-60	
5th Battalion, Malay Regiment (5/Malay Regiment)	1952-60	
6th Battalion, Malay Regiment (6/Malay Regiment)	1952-60	
		(continued on next page)

Table 4. British and Commonwealth Order of Battle, Malayan Emergency

Unit	Deployment Dates	Remarks
7th Battalion, Malay Regiment (7/Malay Regiment)	1952-60	
1st Battalion, Federation Regiment (1/ Fed Regiment)	Sep 1952-60	Formed Sep 52 in northern Malaya
1st Battalion, Fiji Regiment (1/Fiji)	1953-Aug 1956	
3d (Kenya) Battalion, Kings African Rifles (3/ KAR)	Mar 1953-54	
2d (Nyasaland) Battalion, Kings African Rifles (2/ KAR)	May 1953-54	
1st Battalion, Northern Rhodesian Regiment (1/NRR)	1954-56	
2d Battalion, Royal Australian Regiment (2/RAR)	Oct 1955-Sep 1957	Under 28th Commonwealth Brigade
1st Battalion, Royal Australian Regiment (1/RAR)	Oct 1959-Jul 1960	Under 28th Commonwealth Brigade
3d Battalion, Royal Australian Regiment (3/RAR)	Sep 1957-Nov 1958	Under 28th Commonwealth Brigade
1st Battalion, New Zealand Regiment (1/NZ)	Nov 1957-Oct 1959	Under 28th Commonwealth Brigade
2d Battalion, New Zealand Regiment (2/NZ)	Oct 1959-Jul 1960	Under 28th Commonwealth Brigade

180

Table 5. Bosnia—Base Camp Density in the US (MND-N) Sector

	1995	1996	1997	1998	1999	2000	2001	2002	Average
Number of MND-N base camps	43	41	19	18	16	15	13	12	
MND-N base camp density (troops per base camp)	465.10	346.30	747.40	700.00	743.10	450.50	443.10	395.20	536.34
Number of US base camps	33	31	9	8	6	6	6	5	
US base camp density (troops per base camp)	560.60	274.10	944.40	862.50	1033.30	651.10	561.00	570.20	682.15

Table 6. US Forces Deployed to KFOR and MNB-E, 1999-2005

Rotation	Unit	Dates
1A	2d Brigade, 1st Infantry Division (Mech)	June-December 1999
1B	3d Brigade, 1st Infantry Division (Mech)	December 1999-June 2000
2A	1st Brigade, 1st Armored Division	June-December 2000
2B	2d Brigade, 1st Armored Division	December 2000-May 2001
3A	2d Brigade, 101st Airborne Division (Air Assault)	May-November 2001
3B	1st Brigade, 10th Mountain Division (Light Infantry)	November 2001-May 2002
4A	2d Brigade, 1st Infantry Division (Mech)	May-November 2002
4B	3d Brigade, 1st Infantry Division (Mech)	November 2002-March 2003
5A	TF 28th Infantry Division (Mech) (PA ARNG) 56th Brigade, 28th Infantry Division (Mech) (PA ARNG) March 2003-July 2003	July 2003-February 2004
5B	2d Brigade, 34th Infantry Division (IA ARNG)	February-August 2004
6A	37th Brigade, 38th Infantry Division (OH ARNG)	September 2004-March 2005
6B	1st Brigade, 40th Infantry Division (Mech) (CA ARNG)	March 2005-October 2005

182

Table 7. KFOR Command by Nationality

Date	Nationality
June-October 1999	British
October 1999-April 2000	German
April-October 2000	Spanish
October 2000-April 2001	Italian
April 2001-October 2001	Norwegian
October 2001-October 2002	French
October 2002-October 2003	Italian
October 2003-August 2004	German
September 2004-September 2005	French
September 2005-September 2006	Italian
Number of different commanders per brigade, 1999-2005	
MND-E American	13
MND-C British/Swedish (2000) Finnish (2003-04) Czech (2005)	13
MND-N French/MND-NE (after 2002) French	18
MND-S German (1999-2002)	6
MND-W Italian (1999-2002)	8
MND-SW (2002-05) German/Italian	6

Table 8. New York Police Department Organization

Higher Command	Precinct	Area (sq mi)	Population	Command Grade
Patrol Borough Manhattan South (Assistant Chief)	1	1.00	40,451	Captain
	5	1.20	57,199	Captain
	6	0.79	64,355	Deputy Inspector
	7	0.62	58,438	Deputy Inspector
	9	0.79	71,503	Captain
	10	0.93	42,312	Captain
	13	1.08	84,121	Deputy Inspector
	17	0.94	75,063	Deputy Inspector
	Midtown North	1.13	49,984	Inspector
	Midtown South	0.77	16,179	Deputy Inspector
Patrol Borough Manhattan North (Assistant Chief)	19	1.75	217,063	Inspector
	20	1.10	96,865	Deputy Inspector
	23	0.91	72,582	Deputy Inspector
	24	0.91	109,057	Inspector
	25	0.62	45,161	Deputy Inspector
	26	1.00	48,173	Deputy Inspector
	28	0.49	35,500	Deputy Inspector
	30	0.80	64,879	Deputy Inspector
	32	0.98	61,027	Deputy Inspector
	33	1.00	260,000	Deputy Inspector
	34	2.00	123,048	Deputy Inspector
	Central Park	1.31	0	Captain
Patrol Borough Bronx (Assistant Chief)	40	2.80	82,159	Deputy Inspector
	41	2.10	46,824	Captain
	42	1.09	68,574	Captain
	43	4.34	167,663	Captain
	44	1.97	125,000	Deputy Inspector

(continued on next page)

Table 8. New York Police Department Organization

Higher Command	Precinct	Area (sq mi)	Population	Command Grade
Patrol Borough Bronx (Assistant Chief) (continued)	45	8.12	115,960	Captain
	46	1.32	128,313	Inspector
	47	5.50	149,078	Deputy Inspector
	48	No data	75,501	Captain
	49	3.40	111,116	Captain
	50	8.20	101,332	Deputy Inspector
	52	2.00	141,607	Deputy Inspector
Patrol Borough (Strategic and Tactical Command) (Assistant Chief)	73	1.80	85,343	Deputy Inspector
	75	5.50	173,198	Inspector
	77	1.73	96,073	Deputy Inspector
	79	1.20	82,947	Inspector
	81	1.70	60,920	Inspector
	83	2.00	104,358	Deputy Inspector
	84	1.07	43,862	Captain
	88	1.42	98,620	Captain
	90	2.80	104,775	Captain
	94	2.34	55,563	Captain
Patrol Borough Brooklyn South (Assistant Chief)	60	3.40	106,087	Deputy Inspector
	61	5.50	160,319	Captain
	62	3.90	172,222	Captain
	63	8.96	108,325	Deputy Inspector
	66	3.50	185,046	Deputy Inspector
	67	3.40	165,736	Inspector
	68	4.10	122,542	Captain
	69	5.00	85,900	Captain
	70	3.00	168,806	Inspector
	71	1.00	104,014	Deputy Inspector

(continued on next page)

Table 8. New York Police Department Organization

Higher Command	Precinct	Area (sq mi)	Population	Command Grade
Brooklyn South (continued)	72	2.50	120,063	Captain
	76	2.10	43,671	Deputy Inspector
	78	2.20	60,397	Deputy Inspector
Patrol Borough Queens North (Assistant Chief)	104	7.50	167,201	Captain
	108	4.40	109,920	Captain
	109	12.70	242,948	Deputy Inspector
	110	5.50	167,147	Deputy Inspector
	111	9.40	116,404	Captain
	112	3.00	115,910	Captain
	114	6.00	220,740	Deputy Inspector
	115	2.80	169,083	Deputy Inspector
Patrol Borough Queens South (Assistant Chief)	100	3.57	43,584	Captain
	101	2.50	63,154	Captain
	102	5.10	141,814	Deputy Inspector
	103	4.80	101,527	Inspector
	105	12.67	196,284	Captain
	106	6.20	127,274	Captain
	107	7.50	146,594	Deputy Inspector
	113	16.00	122,103	Deputy Inspector
Patrol Borough Staten Island (Assistant Chief)	120	14.10	141,500	Deputy Inspector
	122	27.00	191,090	Captain
	123	17.50	89,772	Captain

Note: 12 transit districts are organized by borough and commanded by a captain.

Table 9. Largest Municipal Police Departments in the United States

City	Population	Area (sq mi)	Size of Police Department	Police Density	
				per square mile	per 1000 population
Houston	2,009,690	579.50	5028	8.67	2.50
Phoenix	1,388,416	474.90	6664	14.03	2.12
San Diego	1,266,753	324.40	1984	6.11	1.58
San Antonio	1,214,725	407.60	2054	5.03	1.69
Dallas	1,208,318	342.60	2833	8.27	2.35
Detroit	911,402	138.80	3645	26.26	4.00
San Jose, CA	898,349	174.90	1320	7.54	1.47
Indianapolis	783,438	361.50	1169	3.23	1.49
Jacksonville, FL	773,781	757.70	1592	2.10	2.06
San Francisco	751,682	46.70	2164	46.33	2.88
Columbus, OH	728,432	210.30	1819	8.64	2.50
Austin	672,011	251.50	1327	5.27	1.98
Memphis	645,978	80.80	2013	24.91	3.12
Baltimore	628,670	279.30	3094	11.07	4.92
Milwaukee	586,941	96.10	1907	19.84	3.25
Washington, DC	563,384	61.40	3782	61.59	6.71

Table 10. Chicago Police Department Organization

Area	District/Station	Sectors/ Beats	Size (square mile)	Population
Central Control Group	1st/Central	3/10	3.14	25,613
	18th/Near North	3/12	4.69	110,995
1st	2d/Wentworth	3/12	3.77	50,967
	7th/Englewood	3/15	6.56	91,600
	8th/Chicago Lawn	3/15	23.12	244,470
	9th/Deering	3/15	13.09	165,457
	21st/Prairie	3/9	4.92	78,111
2d	3d/Grand Crossing	3/12	6.04	93,384
	4th/South Chicago	3/12	27.27	141,422
	5th/Calumet	3/9	12.80	92,729
	6th/Gresham	3/12	8.10	105,360
	22d/Morgan Park	3/9	13.46	111,545
3d	19th/Belmont	3/9	5.57	107,516
	20th/Foster	3/9	4.37	102,512
	23d/Town Hall	3/9	3.01	98,391
	24th/Rogers Park	3/9	5.43	151,435
4th	10th/Ogden	3/12	7.87	137,120
	11th/Harrison	3/15	6.11	82,392
	12th/Monroe	3/9	5.47	69,677
	13th/Wood	3/9	4.21	60,517
5th	14th/ Shakespeare	3/12	6.00	132,459
	15th/Austin	3/9	3.82	72,736
	16th/Jefferson Park	3/12	30.95	199,898
	17th/Albany Park	3/9	9.62	156,859
	25th/Grand Central	3/15	10.91	212,535

188

Table 11. Philadelphia Police Department Organization

Area	District	Area (square mile)	Population
South	1st	**	42,000
	3d		
	South Street Detail		21,178
	4th	6.10	45.566
	17th	1.66	41,328
Northeast	2d		
	7th	13.55	86,500
	8th	14.54	98,146
	15th	8.50	148,000
Northwest	5th	8.51	45,000
	14th		
	35th		
	39th		
Central	6th	2.10	30,000
	9th		
	22d		
	23d		
	Center City		
Southwest	12th		
	16th	1.05*	29,032*
	18th		
	19th		
East	24th		
	25th		
	26th	3.30	54,000
Airport	77th		
Schuylkill	92d		

*Data from 1990, most recent data available
**Areas where information was not available have been left blank.

Table 12. Los Angeles Police Department Organization

Bureau	Division	Area (sq mi)	Popula-tion	Number of Patrol Dist.	Police Patrol Density		
					per area	per pop	per 1000
Valley	Foothills	43.30	182,214	7	8.12	520	1.90
	Devonshire	28.18	201,862	5	12.42	577	1.70
	Mission	53.90	240,000	7	6.49	686	1.50
	West Valley	52.00	300,000	10	6.73	857	1.20
	Van Nuys	30.00	325,000	11	11.70	929	1.10
	North Hollywood	25.00	220,000	10	14.00	628	1.60
	Bureau Total	221.80	1,270,000	50	9.47	605	1.60
West	Hollywood	17.20	300,000	10	20.34	857	1.20
	Pacific	24.10	200,000	8 (+LAX)	14.52	571	1.75
	West LA	65.14	280,000	7	5.37	800	1.75
	Wiltshire	13.97	251,000	13	25.05	717	1.40
	Bureau Total	124.00	840,000	38	11.29	600	1.70
Central	Central	4.50	40,000	6	77.77	114	8.70
	Rampart	8.00	350,000	13	43.75	1000	1.00
	Newton	9.00	150,000	9	38.88	429	2.30
	Hollenbeck	15.20	200,000	7	23.03	571	1.75
	Northeast	29.00	250,000	8	12.06	714	1.40
	Bureau Total	65.00	900,000	43	26.92	514	1.90
South	77th Street	11.90	175,000	11	29.41	500	2.00
	Southeast	10.20	150,000	10	34.31	429	2.30
	Southwest	13.11	165,000	10	26.69	471	2.10
	Harbor	27.00	171,000	8	12.96	489	2.00
	Bureau Total	57.60	640,000	39	24.30	457	2.20
Department total (includes all non-civilian personnel)		466.80	3,694,820	170	19.70	431.2	2.49

Table 13. OIF Troop Deployment by Brigade Equivalent, January 2005

US Forces Deployed	Total of Brigade Equivalents per Command

1st Cavalry Division (MND-B)
  1st Brigade, 1st Cavalry Division
  2d Brigade, 1st Cavalry Division
  3d Brigade, 1st Cavalry Division
  5th Brigade (Provisional), 1st Cavalry Division
  2d Brigade, 10th Mountain Division (Light Infantry) 39th
  Infantry Division (Arkansas ARNG)
  256th Infantry Brigade (Mechanized) (Louisiana ARNG)
Elements, 2d Brigade, 82d Airborne Division
	8

1st Infantry Division (Mechanized) (MND-NC)
  2d Brigade, 1st Infantry Division (Mechanized)
  3d Brigade, 1st Infantry Division (Mechanized)
  2d Brigade, 25th Infantry Division
  30th Infantry Brigade (Mechanized) (North Carolina ARNG)
278th Armored Cavalry Regiment (Tennessee ARNG)
	5

1st Brigade, 25th Infantry Division (Stryker) (MNB-NW)	1
81st Armored Brigade (Washington ARNG) (Theater Security Brigade North)	1
197th Field Artillery Brigade (New Hampshire ARNG) (Theater Security Brigade South)	1

I Marine Expeditionary Force (MNF-W)
  1st Marine Division
    1st Marine Regiment
    5th Marine Regiment
    7th Marine Regiment
2d Brigade, 2d Infantry Division
	4

Coalition Forces Deployed	
South Korean Zaytun Division	1

Polish Division (MND-CS)
  1st Polish Brigade
  2d Ukrainian Brigade
	2

3d United Kingdom (UK) Armored Division (MND-SE)
  4th United Kingdom (UK) Armoured Brigade
  Italian 'Garibaldi' Bersaglieri Mechanized Brigade
  11th Netherlands (NL) Infantry Battalion Battlegroup
	2.25

Total of brigade-equivalents in Iraq, January 2005	25.25

Appendix C

A Special Note on Iraq

The methodology of this work is based on a study of various historical contingency operations at the point of their maximum troop deployment. That information was then used to develop a representative troop density average that could be applied to future planning. The computation of this average, while based on the number of non-indigenous forces deployed for the operation, also included any indigenous forces operational at the time of the maximum deployment strength of the non-indigenous forces as well as any substitute forces, such as contractors, who provided support or conducted missions that released operational forces for other duties.

Using this methodology, the force ratio for the ongoing operation in Iraq was computed for January 2005, the period of the highest troop levels of non-indigenous (i.e. Coalition) forces. The force size, increased to provide security for the Iraqi elections, at that time provided a troop density equation and ratio as follows:

US forces	160,000
Coalition troops (non-US)	24,500
Contractors (estimated)	78,000
Iraqi Security Forces (operational)	0
Total	262,500
Population of Iraq	25.5 million
Ratio 10.29 troops per 1000 local inhabitants	

This yields a troop density ratio lower than the historical average (13.26) found in the six other historical cases of this study (10.29 soldiers per 1000 population versus 13.26 soldiers per 1000).

The Iraqi security forces (ISF) made great progress toward becoming an operational force in the second half of 2004 and had begun to supplement Coalition units during operations. However, in January 2005, no Iraqi forces were independently operational in their own assigned sectors. Accordingly, based on the methodology used in the other case studies in this work, those forces were not included in the computations. Beginning in February 2005, the ISF began to take over operational responsibility for specific areas in Iraq, a process still underway as of the publication of this work.

The operational viability of the ISF in January 2005 is open to debate. As of January 2005, the ISF numbered 124,733 (14,156 army, 36,827

National Guard, 73,750 police). If one includes the ISF in the troop density equation, the result is as follows:

US Forces	160,000
Coalition troops (non-US)	24,500
Contractors (estimated)	78,000
Iraqi security forces (operational)	124,733
Total	387,233
Population of Iraq	25.5 million
Ratio 15.52 troops per 1000 local inhabitants	

This yields a troop density ratio higher than the historical average found in the six other historical cases of this study (15.52 soldiers per 1000 inhabitants versus 13.26 per 1000).

To continue this approach, in September 2005 the formula for troop density, counting the Coalition and ISF forces as they were deployed, is as follows:

US Forces	152,000
Coalition Troops (non-US)	22,409
Contractors (estimated)	78,000
Iraqi Security Forces (operational)	174,409
Total	426,818
Population of Iraq	25.5 million
Ratio 16.73 troops per 1000 local inhabitants	

This yields a troop density ratio higher again than the historical average found in the six other historical cases of this study (16.73 soldiers per 1000 population versus 13.26 per 1000), a higher ratio even as Coalition troop strength was past its peak.

The trend continues to this day. Since September 2005, Coalition forces have remained at roughly the same force levels or declined slightly. However, ISF troop levels have continued to climb and reached a level of 261,500 by May 2006. Additionally, by April 2006, ISF forces were conducting a quarter of all operations independently and another 40 percent of operations in conjunction with Coalition forces.[1]

Since the drafting of this work, two commentaries about troop density have been published reflecting a lower troop density level than cited in this work. In the first of these, the former US Army Chief of Military History, retired Brigadier General John S. Brown, reflected on troop density in past

US occupations and cited as a reasonable ratio one soldier for every 100 inhabitants, or 10 per 1000.[2]

A team of Rand Corporation analysts completed a detailed analysis of post-conflict law and order operations. While including three case studies examined in this work (Bosnia, Kosovo, and Iraq), the Rand team also examined operations in Panama, El Salvador, Somalia, Afghanistan, Haiti, and East Timor. The Rand team has concluded the minimal force required is 1000 soldiers per 100,000 inhabitants or 10 soldiers per 1000 inhabitants. The study also adds a domestic police force of 2 police officers per 1000 of population, giving a combined minimum ratio of 12 soldiers/police per 1000 population.[3]

Notes

1. Anthony Cordesman and William D. Sullivan, "Iraqi Force Development in 2006," (Washington, DC: Center for Strategic and International Studies, June 2006), 32, 83, 109.

2. John S. Brown, "Numerical Considerations in Military Occupations," Army (April 2006), http://www.ausa.org/webpub/DeptArmyMagazine.nsf/byid/ KHYL-6MYKGY, accessed 16 June 2006.

3. Seth G. Jones, Jeremy M. Wilson, Andrew Rathmell, and K. Jack Riley, "Establishing Law and Order after Conflict" (Santa Monica, CA: Rand Corporation, 2005), xiii.

GPO U.S. GOVERNMENT PRINTING OFFICE: 2006—553-266